Praise for the E

Near the end of Thornton Wilder's powerful play *Our Town*, young Emily Gibbs looks down on her village of Grover's Corners, which she is leaving for the last time. In a poignant moment she calls out, "Oh, earth, you are too wonderful for anybody to realize you. Do any human beings ever realize life while they live it—every, every minute?"

Some writers do, and they help the rest of us realize the wonder that surrounds us. Lynn Coffey has that gift, and, once again, she looks down on the hills and valleys of our Blue Ridge Mountains and visits people whose lives otherwise might have gone unrecorded. In sharing her wonder, we are enlightened, uplifted, and entertained by the courage, the humor, the resourcefulness, the strength, and the joy she finds in "plain folks."

—Earl Hamner, creator of *The Waltons*

Like its predecessor, this book is a celebration—of the people and pastimes of a bygone era and a magical place. It is a snapshot of a flickering candle before it burns out, and Lynn Coffey is the keeper of the flame.

—Brad Herzog, best-selling author of the American travel memoirs *Turn Left at the Trojan Horse* and *States of Mind*

Babies and burials, digging ginseng and churning butter, and the art of caning a chair . . . foxfire, beekeeping, log-cabin remedies for lockjaw and freckles, and the way the fog lies on the Blue Ridge in the early morning . . . Lynn Coffey's *Backroads* is a rich appreciation of the mountain way of life, her prose as clear and inviting as any mountain river.

—Lisa Tracy, author of *Objects of Our Affection* and the award-winning *Muddy Waters*

Backroads 2

The Road to Chicken Holler

Lynn Coffey

Quarter Books

Cover design by Jane Hagaman
Cover photo by Lynn Coffey, the road to Chicken Holler
    (Milepost 16 on the Blue Ridge Parkway at Love, VA)
Author photo by Bob Nelms
Interior design by Jane Hagaman
Unless otherwise noted, all interior photos by Lynn Coffey

Quartet Books
PO Box 4204
Charlottesville, VA 22905

If you are unable to order this book from your local
bookseller, you may order directly from the author.
Call 540-949-0329 or use the order form in the back
of the book.

Library of Congress Control Number: 2010911553

ISBN 978-0-615-39241-7

Printed on acid-free paper in the United States of America

Dedicated to the one I love:
"The man from Chicken Holler"

Billy Coffey, Love, Virginia

Contents

Foreword

Communications technology and the misdirected cult of celebrity are moving modern generations of Americans away from the root values of work and responsibility that built the foundations of our country. Fortunately, for the sake of heritage and legacy, we have dedicated documentarians such as Lynn Coffey to preserve our most noble traditions.

In her Backroads series, Lynn Coffey is more than providing insights into the self-sufficiency of the common men and women of Appalachia; she is giving us a means to measure ourselves against the standards of character that the pioneers of our land set for us. What these rural Americans achieved by their own ingenuity and compassion is both remarkable and inspiring. The Backroads individuals whom Lynn recognizes are truly uncommon and worthy of our attention. They are the backbones of our stature through wars and economic depressions. We stand straight and tall today with all the benefits of our society because they did not fail us in their steadfastness.

Few people today know the details of the lives of their grandparents and great-grandparents. In the race to achieve and consume, we have forgotten the huge difficulties of simply enduring what they faced in a country with no social safety net. No matter where your twentieth-century ancestors lived, and regardless of their education levels or material standing, it is the ethic and stoutheartedness of America's rural people that bind us together. We need to know them if we, as Americans, are truly to know ourselves.

Lynn Coffey has gone where we should go in the recovery of our American-ness. She has traveled the back roads to find our indigenous selves and to preserve that legacy in meaningful interviews and story-telling photographs. This is important work for a country that needs to be reminded that where we come from provides a true compass for where we need to go. Our commonly held values should be ageless.

—Monty Joynes
September 2010

Author, artist, screenwriter, and librettist, Monty Joynes wrote *The Celestine Prophecy: The Making of the Movie* with James Redfield, and *Conversations with God: The Making of the Movie* with Neale Donald Walsch, among more than a dozen published books, including the critically acclaimed *Naked into the Night*, the first novel in his Native American–themed Booker series. He lives in the Blue Ridge Mountains of North Carolina with his wife, Pat.

Acknowledgments

As with the original *Backroads: Plain Folk and Simple Livin'*, I am indebted to the special people who believed my work had merit and encouraged me to write a book in the first place. I had no idea I could write *one* book much less *two* books about the Appalachian culture and yet these same folks continued to cheer me on. I gratefully thank each for the part they played in the completion of *Backroads 2: The Road to Chicken Holler*.

For all the dear people who supported *Backroads* newspaper throughout its twenty-five-year existence and then turned around and bought my first published book (and hopefully this one, too!), I have you to thank for making my work so rewarding. To love what you do is a blessing . . . to have *others* love what you do is a double blessing. Thank you for allowing me to have both!

For the four gals who make up Quartet Books, the publishing team that took a chance on an unknown author and used me as their "guinea pig" for their first book project together—all the compliments of how professional the Backroads books look I owe to them. For Tania Seymour, who copyedits the manuscript and scrutinizes my writing with a magnifying glass until it's perfect; for Jane Hagaman, the wizard of layout, who also makes a book cover so eye-popping that people are immediately drawn to it; for Cynthia Mitchell, who proofs the galley with a fine-toothed comb and finds the best prices for printing; for Sara Sgarlat (and her husband Leonard Baker) who is responsible for publicity. All have advised me well, and I respect their combined talents in the publishing field.

For my dear husband, Billy, who not only supported me while I published *Backroads* newspaper, but also stood by me while the first and second Backroads books were being written. When I say, "I couldn't have done it without him," it is not some idle comment. I literally could *not* have done it, because I am totally inept on the computer and even while his mild threats of "you really need to learn how to do this" fall on deaf ears, he continues to do most of my electronic work with typical stoic fashion. God could never have given me a better helpmeet to go through life with. He is a man of endless patience.

And speaking of God, He's the one everyone should thank for the book you are holding in your hands. It was His idea to bring a Florida flatlander to the Blue Ridge Mountains of Virginia to document the lives of the native people who have lived here for centuries. He's the one who blessed me with the talent I needed to accomplish this work and gave me the love for the older mountain people. In a world where so many don't know what God's plan is for them, I thank Him for making it crystal clear to me.

Introduction

For those who are seeing this second Backroads book and somehow missed the first one, I'll give a brief history of how these books about the Appalachian culture came to be.

I, Lynn Coffey, have never been what you'd call a formal writer. In fact, looking back, the only talent I had for what I do has been God-given and even with that advantage, it wasn't much. As a child, I loved to write stuff down on paper and take incessant photographs of everybody I knew with my Brownie camera, although I didn't master the art of not chopping off heads and other body parts in my pictures until later in life. I've always felt I'd been born about a century too late, since I leaned heavily toward the "old ways," even though I was a city girl from south Florida. My city parents wondered where their only daughter fit in the gene pool, because I seemed to be perpetually swimming against the current of typical family flow.

I never did like the heat and humidity of south Florida and when I was little, I told my mother, "I'm going to move to the mountains and live in a log cabin." I remember one vacation our family took when we somehow got off course and ended up on a back road in the hills of Kentucky. My dad was driving our old brown '57 Plymouth station wagon, and I was sitting in the very back with the rear window flipped up, watching the rural sights whizzing by. All of a sudden, Daddy slowed and told me to look up ahead. I saw an old woman driving a herd of pigs right down the middle of the road, and as we inched by, I waved at her. She smiled a big toothless smile, and I proudly announced, "That's what I want to do when I get big!" My mother made a funny snorting sound, and when I looked at her, I noticed her eyes were about to bug out of her head, and she was fanning herself, even though it was cool up there in the mountains.

Long story short, I left Florida the month after my twenty-second birthday and moved to Virginia, where I have made my home for more than forty years. I love the T-shirt slogan, "I wasn't born a Virginian, but I got here as soon as I could!" And basically, that's how it happened.

In 1980, I moved to the tiny hamlet of Love, Virginia (population 82), and couldn't help but notice the Appalachian culture going on around me. My older neighbors, born and raised here, continued to live their lives and do the same activities they had done since childhood. I felt like I had arrived . . . this was the place and these were the people I wanted to spend the rest of my life with.

My neighbor, Bunny Stein, who had moved to Love from Richmond years before, felt the same way; together we started an eight-page newspaper called *Backroads*, which contained interviews with our mountain neighbors and stories of them and their crafts. Before long, word of *Backroads* spread, and we had to add more pages just to keep up with all the "old" news people wanted to read about. Bunny left the paper after the first year, and I continued on solo, asking God to help me write the stories in a truthful and honest way and to bless the people who read it.

When I moved to Love, my goal was to know the names of the people in the cabins that dotted the landscape of the Blue Ridge where I lived. In a few short years, I not only knew their names but also could go to any one of their houses and get a jelly biscuit and a cup of coffee. Such friendships were forged with the mountain people that I didn't know where they left off and I began. I felt my gift to them was to be able to write their stories and histories in a personal, caring manner and to try to dispel the "hillbilly" stereotype that so many people mistakenly apply to them. I found the mountain people to be the most giving, resourceful, talented, kind-hearted folks I've ever known, but they *are* private, and one needs to respect their space.

For twenty-five years, *Backroads* represented the Appalachian culture and gave a voice to the native people whose ancestors pioneered the rugged Blue Ridge chain. When I retired myself and *Backroads* newspaper in December 2006, those same folks encouraged me to do something more permanent with all the material that I had collected through the years. The old newspapers were starting to yellow with age and become brittle to the touch.

During the winter of 2008–09, I sat down and started thumbing through all the old papers, writing down a list of people and subjects I thought would be interesting if put in book form. When enough chapters were compiled, I looked into self-publishing and found four amazing women whose combined talents in the publishing field started the ball rolling. By Thanksgiving 2009, *Backroads: Plain Folk and Simple Livin'* arrived; the boxes stacked to the ceiling of our cabin.

I never thought I'd see the end of those boxes, but by the spring of 2010, they were dwindling. When I started this book project, as with *Backroads* newspaper, I prayed mightily, asking God to bless my work and the people who purchased the book. I told Him wherever He took it, I would follow, even if it meant stepping out of my comfort zone. Boy! What a wild ride book publishing has turned out to be! But it has also been one of the most rewarding things I've ever been a part of.

The success of the first book spurred me on to do a second one, plus the unbelievable winter of 2009–10 afforded me *lots* of time indoors, so I thought I might as well put it to good use! The first book was entitled *Backroads: Plain Folk and Simple Livin'* because that was the newspaper's name and part of its front cover logo. This second book is named *Backroads 2: The Road to Chicken Holler* because the front cover photograph shows exactly that; the winding road down to my husband's homeplace in Chicken Holler. The sixteen-by-twenty-foot cabin in which he was raised was built by his great-grandfather, George Washington "Wash" Coffey in the 1800s, and the land on which it stands has been in our family for at least seven generations. It is still the site of many family get-togethers and I hope it will continue to be for many more generations.

People have overwhelmed me with their positive comments about how much they loved the Backroads book because it took them back to a simpler time when self-sufficiency was the rule. What amazed me most was the younger generation who bought the book and commented on how they wanted to learn to do things like can vegetables, make homemade jelly, or butcher a hog!

One sweet young lady by the name of Derilene McCloud became emotional when she told me that reading the book transported her back to her childhood, when her grandmother raised her in the country. She wistfully remembered her grandma drinking her coffee like Nin Coffey did in the book, by pouring the coffee from the cup into a saucer where it would cool faster, then drinking it from the saucer. And how her grandmother, much like Teressie Coffey, always had an abundance of safety pins attached to her clothing, not to hold the fabric together, but simply because "you never know when you're going to need a safety pin."

The first book, as well as this second one, is meant to not only bring back these pleasant memories but to provide inspiration for doing more for ourselves instead of letting technology take over our lives completely. Just like the inscription I've come to use when signing a book, "The old mountain ways are still the best ways."

Blessings,

—Lynn Coffey

Backroads 2

Doris Hamner at her Schuyler home

1

Doris Giannini Hamner

Schuyler, Virginia

L ooking back to the first *Backroads'* interviews, I shudder to think how bold we were, totally lacking in journalistic protocol. And yet, those were the some of the best articles that Bunny and I did. Those we talked to were forgiving, salt-of-the-earth people who knew as much about proper protocol as we did, thank the good Lord, and they invited us into their homes and let us record their personal histories without hesitation. Doris Hamner was one such woman, and to this day, I have to smile at our first meeting.

Of course, we knew that Doris was the real persona of "Olivia," the mother in the 1970s hit TV series *The Waltons*; her son Earl Hamner, Jr., was "John-Boy." But we had no idea where she lived other than the fact that it was in the little hamlet of Schuyler, Virginia. So, armed with a map of Nelson County, notepad, camera, and a few copies of *Backroads*, Bunny and I set out early one mild spring day in 1982 in search of Doris Hamner for an interview.

Once in the village, we spotted Ike Godsey's Store, a little country grocery that was then being run by a Mrs. Snead. She directed us to a neat, two-story white frame home just down the road and assured us that Mrs. Hamner was home. And no wonder . . . it was just before nine in the morning!

The Hamner homeplace in Schuyler, Virginia. The model for TV's *The Waltons* house.

We walked up to the back porch and knocked on the door. A diminutive nice-looking older woman answered and asked if she could help us "girls." She was dressed in her robe and slippers and was holding a cup of coffee. We told her who we were, showed her a copy of *Backroads*, and asked if we could interview her for the paper. Instead of being put-off or rude, which she certainly had a right to be at that early hour, she flung the door open and invited us in. She asked if we wanted a cup of coffee and a jelly biscuit while we chatted, and the three of us sat down at the kitchen table and proceeded to have the most delightful conversation before the "official" interview began. I found Doris to be a gracious Southern lady, full of wisdom, humor, and kindness. Her soft-spoken Virginia accent only added to her charm, and the conversation revolved around her large family and how proud she was of each of her children.

Here is the interview with Mrs. Hamner as it appeared in the May 1982 issue of *Backroads*. I'd also like to thank the equally gracious Earl Hamner, Jr., for providing the photos of his family, since all my early photographs were lost in a 1986 house fire.

BACKROADS: I hope you don't mind us coming so early in the morning unannounced.

MRS. HAMNER: Oh, no, I don't mind at all. Have you been here before?

BR: No, not exactly. We did come by once a long time ago. You didn't even have the fence up then. It was when *The Waltons* had just begun, and we were so excited about seeing where they lived.

MRS. H: You know *The Waltons* went on for nine years?

BR: Do you still watch it every day?

MRS. H: Oh yes, every afternoon at 4:30.

BR: Has your life changed here in Schuyler because of the series? Do people come up to your door wanting to take pictures and talk to you?

MRS. H: Yes, they come up to my gate, but I keep it locked now because the people were trampling my flowers. Whole busloads come and want to talk, but I can't let them in because my house is so small. So I go out in the yard and talk to them.

BR: Where do these busses come from?

MRS. H: Well, this week I had a huge bus from Greenville, North Carolina, but they come from all over the country.

BR: Tell us about the TV characters. Were they real people from your life, for instance, the Baldwin sisters?

MRS. H: Oh yes, they lived about twenty-five miles from here, down in Albemarle County. These two old ladies were from a very wealthy family. Their house is still standing and is now a home for boys.

BR: How about Ike Godsey?

MRS. H: Yes, he ran the little store up the road, but he and his wife are both dead now, and the lady who runs the store is Mrs. Snead.

BR: How about the black lady who was in the TV series?

MRS. H: Vertie. Yes, there was a lady who lived right close by here, and she was a domestic. She was a dear lady, and my children used to visit her often.

BR: What about that shifty, likable character named Yancey Tucker?

MRS. H: Yes, he was very real but was misunderstood by most people of the area. He grew up an orphan and had no real home of his own. He would do almost any type of chore in exchange for a meal. My husband Earl would occasionally hire him to cut wood for us and then he'd give him fifty-cents or a dollar.

BR: Have you ever had the opportunity to meet the TV characters that played these parts?

Mrs. H: Yes, the last time I was out in California I attended the 200th show of *The Waltons* at this big hotel. It was held in the ballroom, and everybody who had ever been in the series was there. They served supper that night, and it was called the 200th anniversary of *The Waltons*. They served everything home style, such as corn on the cob and hot biscuits.

BR: Mrs. Hamner, let's find out a little more about your side of the family. Where did they come from originally?

Mrs. H: My father came from Italy and was one of the first Gianninis that Thomas Jefferson, who was the ambassador to Italy at that time, brought over to America. They were farmers and knew how to raise grapes and fruit trees. Anthony Giannini was my father's name, and I have one grandson who was named after him. My mother was Irish and had that red hair that we all inherited.

BR: Tell us about your immediate family. Are they all married now except "Jim-Bob"?

Mrs. H: Yes, and "Jim-Bob's" real name is James. "John-Boy" is Earl, Jr., "Jason" is Clifton, "Ben" is Willard; is that five boys?

BR: No, that's only four boys.

Mrs. H: Well I have another son whose name is Paul. "Mary Ellen" is my daughter Marion, "Erin" is Audrey, and "Elizabeth" is Nancy.

BR: How many grandchildren do you have?

Mrs. H: I have sixteen grandchildren and three great-grandchildren and a little grandson that I haven't seen yet who lives in Richmond. Here's a picture of one of my grandsons who stays with me a good bit of the summer. He goes to the Walton School.

BR: Is there really a Walton School?

Mrs. H: Yes, it's near Charlottesville.

BR: Does he like the school?

Mrs. H: Oh yes, he's excited about going there and he says every weekend, "Grandmother, they want you to come over to Walton School and talk to the children." And I say, "Well okay, I'll have to come over there and talk to them real soon."

BR: One of the most outstanding things about the TV series is how the mother maintained her Christian faith throughout the trials and joys of her life. Does this hold true in your real life?

Mrs. H: Yes, I read the Bible every morning and every night, and it still sustains me in my life today.

Br: Do you still attend the Baptist church down around the corner?

Mrs. H: Yes, I still go there, and every one of my children joined that church except Earl, Jr., who joined the St. Stephens Episcopal Church in Richmond after his graduation.

Br: Do you still do your own gardening and canning?

The Hamner family in 1978. From left to right: (back row) Cliff; (next row) Willard, Paul, Jim, Marion, and Nancy; (3rd row) Doris Hamner and Audrey; (front row) Earl

Mrs. H: I still do all my own canning, but I leave the gardening to my son James and my grandson. Last year I had enough string beans and tomatoes to last all year. I have one jar of tomatoes left, and last Sunday I used the last jar of string beans, and all of that came out of my little grandson's garden.

Br: Do you see a big difference in the way children are being brought up as compared to when you brought up yours?

Mrs. H: Oh yes, but I think it's better today, though. Not that they are any smarter than we were when we were coming up, but the children these days are very bright and know what they want. Most of mine knew what they wanted, and they are all doing so well. I'm so pleased with every child that I have.

Br: How has this area changed in the last fifty years?

Mrs. H: It hasn't really changed much. There were dirt roads then, and they were very dusty. We used to call the Lynchburg water company to come and sprinkle the roads to keep the dust down. The people here are still friendly and have time to chat a little.

The Hamner clan when they first moved to Nelson from Buckingham County in 1910.
Earl, Sr., at ten years old, is on the far right holding the duckling.

BR: Where, exactly, is Walton's mountain?

MRS. H: Actually, it's called Wale's mountain, and it's about a mile away from here. My husband used to squirrel hunt there, and my children went up there to find chinquapins and chestnuts. At one time, there used to be a girls' music school at the foot of the mountain, but now the only thing that remains of it is the old chimney.

BR: What are some of your favorite pastimes?

MRS. H: I go shopping regularly with my sister-in-law who lives next door, and I like to work with my flowerbeds. Some Sunday mornings, James and I fry up some chicken and make a picnic lunch and head up to the Blue Ridge Mountains. On many occasions, the whole family gets together to go to a special picnic area on the Blue Ridge Parkway near Humpback Rocks.

BR: Do you ever get up our way at Love for a visit?

MRS. H: Yes, we went up that way once to look around at Wintergreen Resort, but they wouldn't let us in. My son didn't want to force the issue, but when I told them who he was, they welcomed us whole-heartedly. Also, my sister-in-law has land up that way. She used to go up there on weekends to tend a garden and her fruit trees. My children used to go up there with her at different times and on one occasion when she had filled a big box on her front porch with apples, a large bear came to investigate. When they heard a noise outside and opened the door, the big bear was standing there looking at them. She never went back!

BR: Mrs. Hamner, we have enjoyed so much visiting with you and we would like to invite you to come visit us at our homes in Love, Virginia.

After a pleasant morning chat with Mrs. Hamner, we hated to leave but felt like we had taken enough of her time. As we prepared to go, we took one last look around the cozy, immaculate home. The stairway to the upstairs caught our eye, and we thought we heard children's voices echoing softly in the night . . . Good night John-Boy. Good night Erin. Good night Ben. Good night Mama. . . .

Earl Hamner, Jr., sitting on the porch of *The Waltons* set.

A HAND-LETTERED DESCRIPTION OF NIGHTFALL ON WALTON'S MOUNTAIN
By Earl Hamner

Walton's Mountain

"At night across the mountain, when the darkness falls and the winds sweep down out of the hollows, the wild things with their shiny eyes come to the edge of the clearing. At such an hour, the house seems safe and warm, an island of light and love in a sea of darkness. At such an hour, the word home must have come into being, dreamed up by some creature that never knew a home. In his yearning there must have come to mind the vision of a mother's face, a father's deep voice, the aroma of fresh baked bread, sunshine in a window, the muted sounds of rain on a roof, the sigh of death, the cry of a newborn babe and voices calling goodnight. Home---an island, a refuge, a haven---of love".

by Earl Hamner

Bill Wydner at his Amherst mill

2

Grist Mills

Amherst, Osceola, Stuarts Draft, Wade, and Woodson's Mills

Milling has always been an integral part of the mountain people's lives. Mills also benefited the folks who lived in the valley, who had their grain ground at a nearby facility. In years past, flour and cornmeal were the basic staples of cooking, since women made biscuits, hoecake, and cornbread on a daily basis. Today, we buy flour in a five-pound bag, and it will last us a month or more; but before that convenience, the people of the Blue Ridge kept a continuous supply of flour and cornmeal stored in large wooden barrels in the home, so that they could keep their large families fed.

Each little community had a gristmill or two (usually accompanied by a general mercantile store) run by local people. The miller would take a small percentage of the ground meal as payment or give a credit at his store for items that the farmer couldn't produce, such as sugar, salt, and coffee.

In chapter 30, Burgess Coffey tells of her husband, Hercy, running a gristmill in the tiny hamlet of White Rock. The mill used water from the North Fork of the Tye River to power the large waterwheel that ground wheat and corn. I remember Nin Coffey telling me about when she and her husband Johnny lived in a one-room cabin at the end of Chicken Holler. She would put a large sack of dried corn on her horse and ride down the steep mountain path to White Rock to have it ground into meal at Hercy Coffey's mill. She said that on one occasion, the sack of freshly ground meal slipped off the horse on the ride home, and she had a terrible time trying to lift it back onto the saddle. Nin was a small person, and the image of her wrestling the dead weight of a feed sack onto the back of a horse must have been something to see. But Nin was a determined woman, and somehow she got the sack and herself atop the horse and made it up the mountain to home.

Here in Love, Gordon Everitt and his brother ran a mill, as well as a small store that housed the Love Post Office. I remember some of the older folks telling me that on Saturday afternoons, the Everitts would set some time aside for people to bring their buckwheat in to be ground. The old grinding stones from the mill are now resting on the property of John Will Everitt's descendants.

Other familiar mills in the area included Amherst Milling in Amherst, Osceola Mill in Vesuvius, Stuarts Draft Mill in Stuarts Draft, Wades Mill in the Raphine/Brownsburg area, and Woodson Mill in Lowesville. During the years that I published *Backroads*, I was privileged to interview the owners of each of these mills and print the rich histories of each. Although at this writing some of the mills are now closed or the owners are different, their histories remain the same. I have reprinted the articles just as they were when originally published. Wade's Mill was first featured in the January 1983 issue of *Backroads*; Stuarts Draft Mill in August 1987; Osceola Mill graced the cover of the November 1987 issue; Woodson's Mill in October 1994; and Amherst Milling in October 2005. I have listed the mills alphabetically here.

AMHERST MILLING COMPANY
Amherst, Virginia

July 2005 marked the sixty-fifth consecutive year that the Wydner family has owned and operated Amherst Milling Company. Located along Rutledge Creek near the old Amherst train depot, the mill was first referred to in the March 1813 will of James Franklin, who said that upon his death his two daughters would inherit the business. Over the years, the mill changed ownership several times. On December 2, 1881, the executors for the Thompson family sold the mill, then known as "Thompson's Mill" to John Shrader, who, on the same day, sold it to Richard W. Walton who renamed it "Walton's Mill." Next came the Baldock family who, when they started in 1887, began to sell parts of the mill to various family members until, in 1908, Walker Baldock became sole owner. It was known at that time as "Central Mill." Bill Wydner tells the story about how Mr. Baldock got one of his arms caught in some cogs and took his pocketknife and cut off his own arm to free himself. Baldock and his son also operated an ice plant across the road, but when the son left for Richmond, Walker could not manage by himself and was forced to close the mill. Upon Walker's death in 1936, W. A. Miller bought the mill from Baldock's heirs, but in less than five months, the Farmers and Merchants Bank of Amherst assumed ownership.

On July 11, 1940, Richard McKinley Wydner, Sr., who at the time was operating Bunker Hill Mills in Rockbridge County, purchased Central Mill from the bank and assumed ownership, renaming it the Amherst Milling Company. The Wydner family moved into the former miller's brick home when their son Bill was one year old.

There were three sons in the family, all of whom helped in the mill when growing up. Each of the boys eventually left the business to find other jobs, including Bill who served in the military from

The mill as it originally looked

Courtesy of Bill Wydner

1962 until 1964. During that time, he had married Patricia Bunch and had started a family. When he came home from the service, he worked for twelve years for the Division of Forestry, becoming the Chief Forest Warden for Amherst County, Virginia, a position he held until the 1970s.

By then, his father, Richard, was getting older, so Bill returned to the mill full-time, eventually taking over the operation after his dad's death. He has been there ever since. He and Patricia now live in his parents' brick home, and their two daughters, Teresa and Anne, and their families live just down the road. Anne is now the full-time secretary at the mill, just like her father before her. After talking to her young sons, Nathan and Landon, it looks as if there will be a fourth generation of millers in the family. It is clear that the boys love being there.

Three generations at the mill: Bill Wydner, his daughter Anne, and her son Nathan

Coming to Wydner's Mill today is like turning back the clock a hundred years. A vast array of fresh produce, ground meal, animal feed, farm equipment, and small livestock can be found on the front porch, under the trees, and inside the mill itself. Looking around the mill office transports one back to simpler times. Everything from coal oil lamps, stovetop coffee pots, flat irons, men's suspenders, enamel roasting pans, and Happy Jack dog products line the shelves. A sign posted on the wall caught my eye and made me laugh when I read it: "Please do not dust, Scientific Experiment in Progress!" Outside, cages of colorful chickens and rabbits sit under the large shade trees, and the roosters crow in unison.

The waterwheel at Amherst Milling is a metal overshot wheel made by the Fitz Company and fed by the waters of Rutledge Creek. Bill said that this is only the second wheel that has been used to power the mill in its two-hundred-year existence. The first wheel was replaced in the 1950s when its main shaft broke. In 1948, part of the mill burned down when a diesel engine backfired and a spark caught the wall on fire. A new, bigger addition was built after the fire. Over the years, there have been other disasters, such as a flood, which left about three feet of water standing inside the office. But the mill withstood the various calamities life threw at it and has continued to grow and change with the times.

The mill as it looks today

Years ago, the mill employed up to eight employees, and during the 1940s, ran five and a half days a week, twenty-four hours a day to grind wheat that was then shipped in one-hundred-pound bags to Richmond; from there, the flour was sent overseas to feed military troops. At that time, there were two railway depots close to the mill, and trains would bring feed, hay, and fertilizer to the mill door. In turn, the mill would fill boxcars with ground wheat for the federal government (farming was still the number one occupation then).

Today the mill has two other employees besides Bill and Anne. Charles Fitzgerald, who has been a full-time employee for more than twenty-five years, and Bill's brother Dick, who has been helping since his retirement.

Amherst Milling produces white and yellow cornmeal, both plain and self-rising; rye and whole-wheat flour; small amounts of buckwheat and wheat germ; and a three-grain pancake mix—all of which can be bought freshly ground. Bill has all the white flour ground at a smaller mill and then shipped to his Amherst business. They don't grind as much in the hot, humid summer months as they do in the winter because their products contain no preservatives or additives. During the summer, Bill recommends that people store their meal in the refrigerator or freezer to keep it fresh and from getting "buggy."

The mill grinds its own animal feeds for horses, cows, and hogs. They also carry a full line of Purina products, as well as Hunt Club, Ol' Dan, and Tracker dog feeds. Bill says the business could not survive on grain and meal products alone, so he carries a little bit of everything for the backyard and hobby farmers, as well as the larger farming operations.

Bill Wydner loves his work and when asked what the best part of his job is, his eyes well up with emotion as he says, "It's the people . . . talking with the families of the older generation who came here when my father ran the business and meeting new people who come in."

THE OSCEOLA MILL
Vesuvius, Virginia

The old Vesuvius mill known as Osceola has had a rich and varied history over the last 140 years. It has stood firm from the beginning, watching the rise and fall of the milling industry from its lofty vantage point. It remembers the time when area farmers had to stand in line waiting for their grain to be ground, and it watched silently and without complaint as these same men's children gave up farming the family land and drove to the supermarket to buy their flour. It has known the loneliness of lying empty for long periods of time and the joy of being brought back to life by caring families who made their homes under the mill's steep roof and weathered timbers. Just about the time Osceola was thinking about permanent retirement, the old mill embarked on a brand new career uniquely its own.

Although the huge waterwheel at the rear of the building has long since ceased to turn, the simple elegance of the Osceola is now delighting visitors from all over the world who come to stay at the historic mill. For the Osceola is now a beautiful bed-and-breakfast of the highest caliber.

Under the watchful eyes of Paul and Kathy Newcomb, the old mill is once again thriving. The Newcombs found their "dream come true" in July 1986, after an extensive six-month search in which they looked at two hundred properties, covering an area of some forty thousand miles.

Paul was in a high-pressure job and wanted to spend more time with his family, so the Newcombs decided to change their priorities and try to find jobs that they could do from home. Both had a love of old mills and enjoyed staying in bed-and-breakfast inns around the country. Suddenly the idea of combining the two as a family business blossomed. The Newcombs liked the idea of not only living in a restored mill but sharing its history and ambiance with others in a relaxed, family-oriented atmosphere. What they accomplished in less than a year was phenomenal. They added new wiring, new plumbing, a large kitchen, and bathrooms; Kathy's talents as an expert decorator were evident throughout the mill's interior.

When the Osceola opened for business in May 1987, it boasted six bedrooms in the main mill and a separate "honeymoon cottage" that was built in the old mill store just down the road. Across the road from the mill stands the old miller's house, which is in

The Osceola Mill bed-and-breakfast in Vesuvius, Virginia

the process of being restored also. When finished, the old home will house seven bedrooms (all with private baths), a game room, a music room, and a parlor in which guests can relax.

Paul did extensive research in the Rockbridge Court of Records and found much information on the early structure. He found that the creek at the rear of the mill is now called Marl Creek, but at other times it was known as Midway and Steele's Creek. Its headwaters start at the famous McCormick Farm. There were seven mills along this creek from the McCormick Farm down to Osceola, with the first being known as the "upper mill" and the last, the "lower mill." There was also one known as the "middle mill," but no one seems to recall which one it was.

A handwritten contract dated November 12, 1849, between William S. and Thomas McCormick, showed that Thomas bought the mill for two thousand dollars. Thomas is thought to have given the mill it's unique name, since no mention of Osceola was on the 1849 contract; but in February 1867, when Thomas sold the property to a Hugh Lyles, the name was in evidence. No one really knows why he named his mill after a renegade Creek Indian from Alabama.

In November 1870, Hugh Lyles and his wife, Mary, deeded

three acres across the South River to the trustees of Emory Chapel of the Methodist/Episcopal Church South for exclusive religious use. The chapel is still in use today.

In February 1875, Lyles sold the mill property to Z. H. Rawlings for a sum of five thousand dollars. In this deed, the court recorder misspelled Osceola as "Oceola," and the moniker stuck until the Newcombs recorded their deed with the original spelling in December 1986.

On November 4, 1904, Z. H. Rawlings sold the mill and nineteen acres to C. B. Magnus for just two thousand dollars in cash. It was around this time that the mill appeared to reach its peak operation. Over a period of time, C. B. sold all but the mill and 1.6 acres to his brother, Sidney Magnus. In 1931, the mill and house properties were fully separated, with Sidney's wife, Phoebe, running a boardinghouse across from the mill and C. B. operating the mill. Later that year, C. B. married a woman named Mattie and upon C. B.'s death in 1934, the property reverted to her. After Mattie's death, the property went to the Baptist Orphanage in Salem, Virginia. They, in turn, sold it to George Searson in 1948. Searson's family had also owned the "middle mill" for many years. The operation of Osceola proved too much for Searson, so in December 1948, he sold it to A. J. and Beverley Brewbaker for sixty-five hundred dollars.

The Brewbakers operated the mill with reasonable success until the "Flood of 1969." Hurricane Camille wiped out the dam and the water supply. By then, the cost of restoring the essential parts of the milling operation proved too great. This, along with the fact that there was little market for "Flavo" brand products, forced the mill to close its doors.

After that time, the house and mill property was sold to many different families. People such as the Lackeys, Newberrys, Cullens, Claytons, McCalls, and, finally, the Newcombs have made their homes in the old structure or in the miller's house across the road.

From the McCormicks, who no doubt built the mill, to the Newcombs, who now run the bed-and-breakfast, the Osceola Mill continues to live on in proud splendor.

THE STUARTS DRAFT MILL
Stuarts Draft, Virginia

The Stuarts Draft Mill stands alongside the Norfolk and Western railroad tracks at the edge of town. It has had a rich and interesting life since its beginning in 1892. In its ninety-five years of existence, the mill has seen many owners and many changes. Memories linger in the hearts of those people who still remember what it was like to walk to the mill and buy fresh-ground flour for that night's biscuits.

Like so many other early businesses, the mill is now just a shadow of its former self, but it remains an ever-important link to our area's past. Read on as I turn back the hands of time and visit Stuarts Draft when life was simpler, and the mill was in its heyday.

The year was 1892 and Mr. C. H. Cohron was building a new flourmill near the Norfolk and Western railroad line in the blossoming community of Stuarts Draft. When the mill was completed, it continued to be run by the Cohron family.

Stuarts Draft Mill in its early years

In 1917, a fire destroyed the structure. Many of the old mills fell victim to the ravages of fire that, in most cases, were caused by spontaneous combustion. The mill wasn't reconstructed until 1922 when C. H. Cohron's two sons, Pilson and Alvin, decided to rebuild it. Pilson felt it would be bad luck to rebuild on the same spot, so the new mill was reconstructed a little farther up the railroad tracks. The two brothers operated the mill for another twenty-four years before selling it to W. I. Grove in 1936.

Grove owned three other area mills: one in New Hope, one in Elkton, and one in Mount Crawford. He wanted the Stuarts Draft Mill as a "backup" for when his other mills could not produce enough. He continued to operate the mill until 1946, when his son, W. W. "Bill" Grove, bought it and developed it into a business of his own.

I interviewed one of Bill Grove's sons, Bobby, and he provided me with a wealth of information concerning the mill itself and some warmhearted remembrances of what it was like growing up in his dad's business.

In the early years, the mill produced fifty or more products, flour being one of the mainstays of the business. At one time, there were sixteen to eighteen employees, and the mill produced about seventy-five thousand pounds of flour a week. All told, the Stuarts Draft branch made nine separate brands of flour. Although the bag names were different, the flour inside was the same. The point was argued upon by the people who used one brand over another and swore it tasted better. The reason behind having so many brand names was that each store that carried the flour wanted an exclusive name-brand flour for their business. So names like "Good as Gold," "Famous Rose," "Nor-So-Na," "Flavo," "Cream of the Harvest," "Peacock," and "None Better" flooded the shelves of local markets.

Animal feeds made up the rest of the mill's sales. Flour and animal

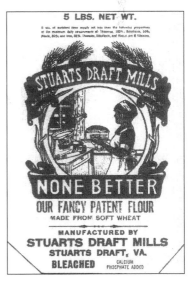

One of Stuarts Draft Mill's flour bags

feed were milled separately, each in its own building. Horse, cattle, and hog feeds were made, as well as chicken scratch. In later years, dog food was also sold at the mill.

At harvest time, Mr. Grove bought all the wheat the area farmers could provide him with. He, in turn, would grind the grain and resell it at the mill or along the different routes established in Middlebrook, Monterey, McDowell, Craigsville, Goshen, and Augusta Springs. Bobby Grove remembers riding the route with driver Bob Tillman (whose wife, according to Bobby, made the best egg salad sandwiches!).

"We'd stop at all the little gas and grocery stores along the way," recalls Bobby with a grin, "and deliver flour in everything from two-pound bags to one hundred-pound sacks."

Back then, there were three route salesmen employed by the mill. Their job was to make contacts at these small grocery stores and take orders for fresh ground flour. The three salesmen were Charlie Rimer, Hugh Hall, and a Mr. Allen. There were also several mobile mills that were transported to neighboring farms, and people could get their grain ground "on the spot." The operators of these mobile units were G. T. Almarode and Erby Loan. They would take molasses and other concentrates with them and mix it in with the farmer's grain to make a more palatable animal feed.

There were two flour-bagging machines at the mill then. One for twenty-five-, fifty-, and one-hundred-pound bags and a smaller one for two-, five-, and ten-pound bags. The twenty-five-pound paper bags were tied with a cord while the fifty- and one-hundred-pound bags were made of heavy cloth and stitched shut. The two-, five-, and ten-pound bags had to be glued shut. As young children, Bobby and his brothers Kirk and Billy, Jr., were well versed in the bagging/gluing process. And they were all involved in the continual job of "sweeping up." But the work was balanced out by a bit of childhood fun, which ranged from shooting rats in the mill basement to playing between the tile grain silos and riding the belt elevator up the four stories of the mill.

Bobby had all sorts of memories about growing up around the mill. When he was in the first grade, he remembers that his parents came to get him at school and took him to New Hope where his Uncle Jimmy's grain mill was on fire. It happened again when he was in the third grade, and the Mount Crawford Mill was on fire. "I remember standing there and watching them burn to the ground," said Bobby. But not all the memories were tragic. Some of the more pleasant ones involved watching the "Plain People" (Amish) coming to the mill in their horse-drawn wagons and buggies. The community of Stuarts Draft was quieter then and more conducive to the Amish way of life.

But time was moving on, and, in 1970, Bill Grove knew his business was in danger of becoming extinct. The once-modern equipment of belts and pulleys, which were run by a huge electric motor and much manual labor, was largely outdated, and he felt it was time to get out of the milling trade. So the business was sold to the Augusta Farm Bureau. A man by the name of Phillips ran the mill for the Farm Bureau. They continued operation until April 18, 1980, when they decided to lease it. At that time, Sonny Wheelbarger and Lee Hutchinson were working for Dayton Feed Company, which was located in the old Ballew building close to the railroad tracks in Stuarts Draft. Despite a difference in ages, the two worked well together. They made a move to another feed company, then decided to lease the Stuarts Draft Mill.

By turning the mill's production into strictly animal feeds, Sonny and Lee turned the business around, and it began to flourish. They bought the mill in 1982, but a year later, the upper stories started to deteriorate so badly that the decision was made to tear down three stories and leave the bottom floor for office space. I remember taking a picture of the old structure before it was taken down. Many of the mill relics were given away to various people, but some of them still grace the interior of the feed store office.

As of August 1987, the mill is still thriving under the watchful eyes of Sonny Wheelbarger and Lee Hutchinson. Computers have replaced the antiquated machinery and their capabilities are endless. Sonny says that they are now able to compute ration balancing for each farm, figuring out how much feed is necessary per animal based on forage analysis and milk-production levels.

The mill in the early 1980s, before the upper stories were removed

The mill has seen a lot of changes in its lifetime, and it is truly amazing that after ninety-five years, it continues to thrive. Sonny predicts the mill will be in production for another century or two, and I told him I'd be around in about fifty years or so for an update. He said he'd mark it on his appointment calendar. . . .

WADE'S MILL
Raphine, Virginia

Located in Rockbridge County, Virginia, Wade's Mill lies a little to the west of Raphine on Route 606, a beautiful rural area that makes a perfect setting for the famous landmark. Built around 1750 by Joseph Kennedy, the merchant mill played an important part in the economic structure of the area. A merchant mill differs from a gristmill in that it received grain from local farms, which was ground and resold. Gristmills were, for the most part, for people who brought in their grain to be ground for their own home use.

James F. Wade purchased the mill in 1882 after it had been

completely restored following a fire in 1873, which had leveled the huge building. He also bought the old Kennedy homeplace, a large brick structure, which stands a little to the south of the mill. James learned the milling trade from his father-in-law, who was a mill owner in Nellysford. In about 1924, James's son, Walter, took over the milling operation and made several improvements. One of these improvements was a new metal waterwheel to replace the wooden one.

After the World War II, Charles Winston Wade took over his father, Walter's, business and continued to run it as flour and feed mill until 1964, when it became almost impossible to make a living at the old trade. He closed the mill and it sat idle for about thirteen years before he and his son, Charles, Jr., planned a major renovation. But the untimely death of the elder Wade made it too hard a project for someone to do single-handedly. By this time, Charles, Jr., was running the whole operation, in addition to trying to promote his product and deliver the goods.

Due to insufficient profits, Charles had to close the mill and seek employment elsewhere. During this time, a happy coincidental meeting between Charles Wade and the Newcombs of Osceola Mill resulted in a project that not only provided Charles with some money to reopen the mill but saved a portion of our Shenandoah Valley history: the incorporation of Wade's Mill products in the old Flavo bags that Osceola once produced. So once again, the natural, nutritious products of Wade's Mill became available at the Vesuvius bed-and-breakfast.

However, Charles was still struggling financially. Just when he thought it would get the best of him, he met David Beebe, who helped him get back on his feet. The long-awaited renovation could finally begin, and David, who helped Charles run the mill, was in on the project, which took place from September 1981 until February 1982. During that time, a new dam, millrace, and equipment were acquired, along with a major cleanup of the mill itself.

Wade's Mill in 1983, after the renovation

The fifth-generation miller and his friend were the only ones running the old mill, with occasional part-time help for bagging the flour. The huge twenty-one-foot waterwheel is powered by Kennedy Creek, which is located half a mile away. From the dam, the water runs though a race and into a large pipe that rises some twenty-two feet in the air where it empties into a wooden reservoir before falling over the massive wheel. Because the water source is higher than the pipe, the whole operation is gravity fed, thus eliminating the need for a pump.

The main product of the mill was finely ground flour, which came as all-purpose flour, whole-wheat, and natural white-bread flour. The mill also ground cornmeal and buckwheat that was sold in area stores. Stone-ground flour is just that—ground on a one-hundred-year-old French millstone, which actually came with the original mill. The advantage of using stones over rollers, which is what most flour is ground on today, is the high nutritional value and nut-like flavor that result from milling the old way. Because of its coarse texture, bread, rolls, and other baked goods have smaller air bubbles, making the texture firmer and the dough rise higher. This is accomplished by using hard wheat, which is bought from the Midwest. For lighter, fluffier products, such as cakes, biscuits, and pastry crusts, soft wheat is used. This type of grain is bought locally.

Charles Wade and David Beebe ran the mill until 1991, when it was purchased by Jim and Georgie Young in September of that year. The Youngs moved into the miller's house and continued to grind on weekends while additional renovations to the mill took place. The new mill owners continue to carry on the milling tradition of the Kennedy/Wade families, offering fresh stone-ground grains and mixes in various sizes. A large selection of products are available, such as all-purpose flour, whole wheat pastry flour, grits, semolina flour, cracked wheat, muffin mixes, pancake mixes, naturally white and whole-wheat bread flour, and cornbread and biscuit mixes. The Youngs have gift boxes available or will put together a custom box from your choice of products. The Youngs also offer a huge selection of kitchenware on the downstairs floor of the mill and an "International Shop," featuring items from France and Italy as well as other countries around the world, on the second floor. They host a variety of cooking classes and special events.

Wade's Mill continues to grind today just as it did in 1750 when Joseph Kennedy first built it. For that reason alone, it's worth a trip to pastoral Raphine to see for yourself just how flour is produced.

The mill as it looks today

WOODSON'S MILL*
Lowesville, Virginia

A few short years ago, Woodson's Mill was one of too many dilapidated-and-dying Virginia water mills. Since 1972, when first we learned of its existence, my colleagues and I have watched this once-proud, four-story structure slump further and further into decline with each visit. Now the old mill has new life and breath again—the only one of its kind operating in Nelson County, and one of the few double overshot grist mills in the nation. Regrettably, five other mills still standing in this same area are fast following the path that, until recently, Woodson's Mill had trod.

Originally constructed in 1794 by Guiliford Campbell, the mill was rebuilt in 1845, then purchased in 1900 by Julian B. Woodson, MD. "Doc Woodson's Old Mill," as it was referred to locally, became an industrial center through expansion and modernization that began in 1904.

Through the years, flour and cornmeal, feed, lumber, cider, and ice were all produced at Woodson's. Across the road from the main complex were a stable and foundry and, later, a steam-powered sawmill. Woodson also owned a three-thousand-tree apple orchard, a 650-acre farm, and a machine shop—all on the mill property. He had an office in the mill where he practiced dentistry and family and veterinary medicine. All in all, Dr. Woodson was quite a multifaceted gentleman!

Today, the mill has two overshot wheels; but in Woodson's time, a third operated the sawmill and, later, the ice plant. The foundation for a fourth wheel, whose use is now unknown, also stands in a creek which runs through the property.

Following the death of Dr. Woodson (state senator, as well as mill proprietor and medical doctor) in July 1963, the mill lay idle for three years: the wooden teeth having been stripped from the main gear by an inexperienced successor to longtime miller Edd Willis. (To repay a loan from Dr. Woodson, Willis, as a young

---

*The Woodson's Mill article originally appeared in the spring 1987 edition of *Old Mill News*, which was written by Chris Anderson, assisted by J. Gill Brokenbrough, Jr.

man, went to work as a miller, and there he remained for sixty years!)

In 1966, H. T. Campbell purchased the mill property, using the smaller wheel to pump water to his reservoir. Over the years, a number of people offered to buy the mill machinery, but the far-sighted Mr. Campbell always refused, hoping that a subsequent owner might restore the place.

Woodson's Mill as it looked in the 1970s

In 1983, the present owner, J. Gill Brokenbrough, Jr., of Norfolk, Virginia, hired Steve Roberts of Massie's Mill, Virginia, to paint the roof at Woodson's. Steve then suggested clearing years of accumulated junk from the building and doing a general clean up. Practically before they knew it, Gill and Steve had made the decision to proceed with a total restoration. Prior to this, the dam, which is on the Piney River, had been prefabricated (poured all the way to the bedrock), and the race was cleared to allow water to again enter the three-acre pond, which lies downhill from the imposing stone house which is the property residence.

Steve and a crew of three went to work putting up new wood siding, replacing windows, and installing a new sill at the east end of the mill, thus averting an imminent collapse of that wall. Persimmon wood was used to fashion new teeth for the stripped main gear, and the two runs of stones and housings were cleaned and dressed like new. The roller mills, which were cleaned for display, would not be used as part of the mill operation.

One of the biggest problems was refurbishing the 12.5-by-8-foot Fitz overshot wheel, the lower third of which was virtually destroyed by water that had backed up in the tail race. To further complicate things, the header tank and flume were completely gone.

Gill had the wheel sent to a firm in Lynchburg, Virginia, where it was, for all intents and purposes, completely rebuilt along the design of the old Fitz wheel. A Norfolk firm, using old photographs and drawings as guidelines, fabricated the header tank and metal flume.

The smaller wheel at the west end of the building (a copy of a Fitz that the shrewd doctor thought too expensive to buy) was built at Woodson's Foundry. Although a pipe carried water to the wheel, a header tank was added to allow control of the water flow from inside the mill. Keeping to tradition, this header tank was built by the miller and helpers in the mill workshop. This wheel is now operating and is used to generate electricity.

The mill after its restoration

Concrete poured into the original stone-lined race carries the water flow from the picturesque pond to each end of the mill. The double tail race, in turn, carries it under Route 778 and back into the Piney River just below Lowesville.

What experts informed Gill Brokenbrough would require ten years to accomplish has instead taken only three—largely, he insists, thanks to the untiring efforts of Steve Roberts. Their wish is to have not only a restored mill as a museum, but to have a living, working mill, usefully providing service as it has for nearly two hundred years.

Skillet cornbread with homemade butter and honey

3

Cornmeal Recipes

Favorites from Amherst Milling

These four cornmeal recipes came from Bill Wydner, owner of Amherst Milling Company in Amherst, Virginia. I've tried all four and can vouch for their deliciousness!

BOSTON BROWN BREAD

1 cup sour milk

1 cup molasses

1 egg

1 level teaspoon salt

1 level teaspoon baking soda

1 cup sifted cornmeal

2 cups whole-wheat flour

1 cup (or ½ cup each) well-floured nuts or raisins (optional)

Mix ingredients in order listed and put batter into buttered round can set in a large pot of boiling water that reaches one-third the way up on the can. Steam for two and a half to three hours. Coffee cans make good molds for steaming the bread. The bread is especially nice for sandwiches or Sunday night tea.

SPOON BREAD

2½ cups boiling water

2 cups cornmeal

2 eggs (separated)

2 tablespoons melted shortening

1½ teaspoons salt

1½ cups buttermilk

1 teaspoon baking soda

Preheat oven to 450 degrees. Stir cornmeal gradually into boiling water. Let stand until cooled. Dissolve the baking soda in the buttermilk. Beat the egg yolks and stir into the cornmeal, along with the shortening, salt, and buttermilk/baking soda mixture. Stiffly beat the egg whites and add. Dollop large spoonfuls onto a cookie sheet, and bake for forty minutes.

CORNMEAL MUFFINS

1 egg

3 teaspoons baking powder

⅓ teaspoon baking soda

salt (to taste)

1 level tablespoon sugar (optional)

1 cup buttermilk

½ cup flour

1 cup plain cornmeal

Preheat oven to 450 degrees. Beat egg; add baking powder, baking soda, salt, and sugar (if used). Add a small amount of buttermilk and beat together. Add flour and meal and mix with enough buttermilk to make a soft batter. Fill well-greased muffin tins two thirds full and bake for twenty minutes.

CORNMEAL MUSH

2¾ cups
boiling water

1 cup stone-
ground cornmeal

1 teaspoon salt

1 teaspoon sugar

1 cup cold water

Combine cornmeal, salt, sugar, and cold water in a separate bowl. Gradually add this mixture to the boiling water, and cook until batter begins to thicken, stirring frequently. When thick, cover, turn heat to low, and cook for twenty to twenty-five minutes.

Vera Falls working on a quilt

4

Quilting

Upon moving to the Blue Ridge Mountains, I began to notice that there was always a common thread woven into the older women's conversations. Invariably the talk would center on handiwork, quilting in particular. I would listen with interest as Nin and Eva Coffey related how they would finish their everyday work around the cabins and look forward to lowering their quilting frames to work on some colorful new pattern they had started.

In the past, the mountain women had no electricity for television and such, so they relied on old-time crafts to keep their hands occupied and their hearts fulfilled. Quilting not only provided intimate company with other women but also provided families with warm coverings for the winter months. And there was a certain satisfaction in piecing the different color combinations together into something that was uniquely their own. After Nin died, our family bought her and Johnny's home; in the attic, we found bags stuffed with cut quilt pieces.

The chapter photo to the left shows Vera Falls, stitching away on one of the many quilts she has made in her lifetime. Vera said she learned the art as a young teenager from her grandmother, Nannie Coffey. When asked what the first pattern was that she worked on, Vera said it was a "crazy quilt" made up of different colors and fabrics cut out of old clothing. We think that recycling is a new trend, but the mountain people were way ahead of their time in the reuse of many everyday materials. Some of Vera's favorite quilt patterns include the "Rail Fence," "Wedding Ring," "Two-Patch," and her personal favorite, the "Monkey Wrench," the design she's made most often. Although quilting can be a solitary, individual craft, Vera said she enjoyed sewing with her sister Vivian Allen and also Margie Ramsey and Daisy Demastus. They would spend the day together, talking as they stitched away. Vera and Vivian, who often worked together on a single quilt project, made the colorful "Rail Fence" quilt that Vera showed us on the day we came out to take her picture.

The ladies of the Mountain View Mennonite Church would get together one day a week to work around a large frame stretched with a new quilt. As the old adage says, "Many hands make light work," and before they knew it, there was a beautiful quilt to be given to someone in need—a new mother or as a donation to the Relief Sale held in the fall of each year. Ladies from the Mennonite/Amish faiths worked on these quilts all year, and the monies collected from the sales went to the various aid organizations. Watching these women sew was like watching a precision machine as they made perfect tiny stitches. They invited me to come and learn, but after one look at my large, haphazard stitches, they put me on the "cut-out" table. My dear friend Gladys Coffey, tactful as ever, said my true talents lay elsewhere.

Speaking of Gladys, she was one of the most talented quilters I've ever met. Like Nin and Eva, Gladys always had her quilting frame set up with colorful, intricate patterns taking shape. There's no telling how many quilts Gladys made in her lifetime. I know that one Christmas, she made quilts for all four of her children, and most of the grandchildren received one as a wedding present. One Christmas, Gladys's daughter-in-law Sharry returned the favor by making Gladys and her husband, Boyd, a quilt depicting the different phases of their lives. Gladys was thrilled and displayed the quilt with pride.

Betty, Carol Jean, and Judy, Gladys's three daughters, honored me when they presented me with the last quilt their mother made before her death in July 2007. It is a beautiful appliquéd quilt of pastel flowers on a pale green background that was laid across her casket in place of the traditional spray of roses. I treasure it more than the girls will ever know, and each time I see it, in my mind's eye I see Gladys stitching away.

Hazel Fitzgerald of the Beech Grove community was always one of my favorite people to visit. I'd stop by on my way home from delivering *Backroads* newspaper to give Hazel a copy, and she'd talk about growing up here on the mountain. One day, as I was preparing to leave, she called me into her bedroom to give me something she had made. It was an intricate "bow tie" pattern quilt in all my favorite colors; I still use it today.

In the February 1993 issue of *Backroads*, I interviewed Patsy Weaver of Stuarts Draft, who is one of the most avid quilters I ever made acquaintance with. She gave me a wealth of information about how she got started making quilts and the personal satisfaction it brings her. As a small child, Patsy learned the art of quilting from her grandmother, who gave her little jobs of threading needles and handing her pieces of material when she needed them.

Patsy Weaver quilting at home

When she was five years old, her grandmother began teaching her how to piece, and from that time on, Patsy made quilting a lifelong hobby.

Her formal introduction to quilt making came at eighteen years of age when she married Jason Weaver and began attending the quilting bees held at her church. That's when enjoyment of the craft became her passion. The Weavers' home is filled with beautiful quilts that Patsy has made, along with heirloom quilts that have been in their family for generations. Patsy showed me a woven wool coverlet that is more than 125 years old and two quilts made for her and Jason's wedding by their mothers. Jason's mother made a "Double Wedding Ring" pattern that was pieced together from some of his sister's childhood dresses. Patsy's mother fashioned a "Dresden Plate" quilt out of Patsy's sister's clothing.

Patsy says that the trick to a good quilting stitch is to have at least eight to ten uniform stitches per inch. Usually, the greater the number of stitches per inch, the better the quilter. "And the mark of a good quilter," laughs Patsy, "is someone who has one in a frame, is piecing or appliquéing one, cutting one out, buying material for another and has ten patterns in her head!"

In this fast-paced world, many women simply do not have time to do hand stitching, but Patsy adds, "People are tired of things that don't last. They want to get back to the old traditions that really mean something . . . that has a part of someone tied to it."

In the January 1983 *Backroads*, Bunny Stein wrote a wonderful article about quilting that provides even more background to the age-old craft of making "bed covers." I am honored to reprint it here.

Centuries ago, to have any kind of material, it first had to be grown, spun on a wheel, and placed on a loom to be woven into a piece of cloth. No one who had to go through this process ever forgot the enormous amount of work that went into its creation.

During the olden days, the piecing and patching of fragments was considered a sign of thriftiness, and with this innate respect for the value of material, many women unconsciously developed into "artists in scraps."

Since bedding took a primary place as a necessity in the home, the scrap bag was filled with carefully sorted rags, the best ones to be used for quilts while the rest were cut into strips to make rag rugs. After the urgent necessity of supplying adequate bedcovering for the family was fulfilled, the making of quilts for display evolved into an artistic outlet for women with ingenious minds and clever fingers.

The "crazy quilt," the earliest type made, was not considered a design. These quilts were mere constructions of leftovers. When enough pieces were collected, they were sewn together in a mosaic fashion, resulting in a useful covering that would last for centuries. These quilts were constant reminders of the clothes that each member had worn or of an old tablecloth or some worn out curtains because they were all part of the mosaic design.

Bunny talked to Daisy Fitzgerald of Reeds Gap and learned that because her family lived in a remote area where material was not only hard to come by but too costly to buy, they coveted every scrap of fiber that wasn't in use. They saved every piece they could find to make quilts. Daisy said that many times, there would be an exchange of fabrics among friends and relatives. "Piece bags" would be brought out and passed around from hand to hand and traded so that each person could add some color and variety to their patterns.

Small girls learned early in life how to sew and piece a quilt. They learned much about style, color, and design, but they also learned the infinite lesson of patience as they sat quietly for many hours alongside mother and friends. In this activity, a girl was creating a thing of beauty and usefulness, which I'm sure gave her a great deal of satisfaction. As girls got older, they began to think about their dowry, and no girl would dream of getting married before she had prepared an ample supply of quilts for her home.

There are two techniques for making quilts: piecing, like the crazy quilt, and appliqué. Both can be combined on the same article. To appliqué, a shape is designed on a plain background, then patches of material are cut out and hemmed down. This technique allows a big variety in design. The stitching technique known as "quilting" is the sewing of a running stitch along a previously marked out line to unite the several layers of cloth that makes up the quilt, such as the top, the filling, and the bottom. The designs of quilt stitches range from straight to elaborate scrolling, floral, and leaf designs.

Before any of this elaborate needlework can be done, however, the patterns must be marked out, appliquéd, then the whole finished top, along with the filling and backing, must be put on a quilting frame. This is made of wood and constructed somewhat like curtain stretchers (if any can remember those!). These frames can be adjusted to the size of the quilt. The quilt must then be basted or pinned onto a heavy piece of canvas or cloth already attached to each bar of the frame.

Quilting was an occupation usually saved for the winter months when preparations for providing the winter food store were behind and there were fewer demands on the woman's time. Once the daily chores were all done, out would come the quilting frame, which would be set up in a warm corner of the house. When not in use, the frame was frequently raised up into the rafters out of the way.

No woman quilted alone if she could help it. In the old days, when there were fewer social activities, the women would get together at a "quilting bee," which was a form of entertainment at

The ladies from the Pilgrim Fellowship Church in Stuarts Draft, working on a new quilt

which the hostess, in exchange for one or two good meals, received the pooled needlework of a group of her friends.

Quilts are one of the most popular needlework arts in America. The creative use of quilts is unlimited. They are used as wall hangings, pictures, clothing, and even to reupholster furniture and make into pillows and stuffed toys.

The women of old did most of this piecing of quilts by hand. Then the sewing machine came along, which made sewing easier but destroyed some of the craftsmanship and pride in a work made by one's hands. The machine age took over, and store-bought material replaced the spinning wheel and loom, which were resigned to the attic along with the coalscuttle and rolling pin.

But there are women today who still sew by hand and have revived the old craft of quilt making, spinning, and weaving. They are producing some of the old patterns, which seem to be the most popular at present. If a woman can follow the printed word and hold a needle, she can achieve a reasonable facsimile of her grandmother's quilt—if not quite as good.

A pan of lye soap in the making

5

Making Old–Fashioned Lye Soap

Lelia Patterson, Stuarts Draft, Virginia

One hundred years ago, lye soap was one of the essentials of basic living here in the Blue Ridge Mountains of Virginia. In the fall, during butchering time, the fat from the hog was saved and rendered down in a big iron pot that usually stood in the backyard. After the lard was boiled down, it was put into containers and stored for baking purposes or for making a big batch of lye soap.

In the early days, people made their own lye by leaching out the fireplace ashes with water. The end result was lye so strong that it could dissolve a chicken feather, which was the true test of strength. But as the years progressed, Red Devil lye could be purchased in a can from a nearby general store.

I had always wanted to learn how to make this type of soap and perhaps write an article about it in *Backroads*, so when Betty Hodge called and asked if I'd like to watch her mother make a batch, I jumped at the chance. Lelia Patterson of Stuarts Draft has always made her own soap from scratch, and for the December 1985 issue of *Backroads*, she was kind enough to demonstrate how it was done.

The basic recipe for making lye soap is pretty simple. Lelia used two and a half pints of cold water, five pints of warm grease (lard), one can of Red Devil lye, and one pint of Clorox bleach.

Before starting, Lelia gave some helpful hints on what one

should know before making soap. First off, be sure to use an enamel or glass pan or dish to put the lye water in. Lye is very caustic and will eat through other types of material, such as metal or plastic. For this same reason, use wooden utensils, such as a wooden spoon, for stirring. Extreme caution should be used when handling lye. Grandma Patterson rubbed grease all over her hands and arms as well as mine so that the lye wouldn't burn our skin if it accidentally splashed. She explained that even the fumes could burn if you get too close. She also said that the best place to make the soap is on a cool back porch or maybe outside, since the lye water has to cool before mixing the melted lard in.

Lelia and her daughter Betty making lye soap

Okay, here we go. Lelia put two and a half pints of water into a shallow, rectangular enamel pan and very slowly added the canned lye to it, stirring constantly. It got very hot and steamed up. Be sure not to breathe in any of the fumes because it could burn your lungs. Then she continued stirring until the lye dissolved. When the liquid cooled down, Lelia added warm lard slowly to the lye/water mixture and stirred it until it started to thicken up. One-pint of bleach was added to the mixture as Lelia continued to stir. Pretty soon, the soap started to set up. When this happened, Lelia took a knife and marked out where she wanted to cut the soap after it had set up by pressing it lightly with a knife blade. This makes it easier to cut when the soap is finished. Lelia said it only takes a day or two for the soap to harden up and be ready to use.

Lelia stirring the ingredients

The uses for lye soap are numerous. There's nothing better to get the collar stains off a white shirt. Simply wet the soap and rub directly on the collar before washing. The older mountain people also grated some of the soap and used it as you would commercial detergent, right in the wash water. Even though you'd think that with the lye being so strong, it would be rough on the hands, but women who have used the soap said it made their skin very soft to the touch. I've found there is nothing better for cutting the oil of poison ivy once you've been exposed or drying up the itch after you've contracted it. And, of course, it has always been a standard for washing out the mouth of young children who have let a forbidden word slip into their vocabulary. . . .

OTHER RECIPES FOR LYE SOAP

Imogene Kurtz from Staunton, Virginia, provided this recipe for making lye soap.

3 cups warm water

1 can Red Seal lye

6 pounds lard

2 tablespoons sugar

2 tablespoons powdered borax

½ cup clear ammonia

Pour the lye slowly into the water. While it's still warm, slowly add the melted lard. Stir for ten minutes and then add the sugar, borax, and ammonia. Stir until creamy. Let set up before making marks to cut for the size of cakes. Take out and let cure. Be sure to use an enamel pan and a wooden spoon for stirring.

Beth Hodge Wright of Calf Mountain Road uses this recipe, which came from a book called *The Art of Soapmaking,* by Merilyn Mohr. It is a mild-complexion soap, and the recipe is very simple.

4 cups clean lard

1 cup Crisco oil

4 tablespoons (½ cup) Vaseline

2 cups cold, soft water

½ cup plus 2 teaspoons lye flakes

Spray a 9.5-by-11-inch enamel or glass pan with Pam or just grease it with some lard. Melt the four cups of lard in a saucepan and add more if the melted amount doesn't quite equal four cups. Stir in the Crisco and then add the Vaseline. Put the two cups of soft water in a separate enamel pan. Using a wooden spoon, stir in the lye flakes. Be careful, this mixture gets really hot! When the lard temperature reaches 85 degrees and the lye temperature reaches 75 degrees, slowly pour the lye water into the fat mixture. You can use a candy thermometer to measure the exact temperature. To hasten the cooling process, place both the fat and the lye pans in an ice bath in your sink. Just watch them carefully, and when each is at the correct temperature, they can be mixed.

If you'd like to add a special fragrance to the soap, now is the time to do it.

You can find little bottles of oil in candy stores, with scents such as clove, cinnamon, lemon, or wintergreen. About twelve drops of oil should give the soap a nice smell. Using sassafras oil gives the soap a unique fragrance that everyone loves but can't quite identify.

After the lye water is poured into the fat, continue to stir until the wooden spoon can stand alone in the middle of the pan. Quickly pour the mixture into the greased baking dish and smooth out flat. Put in a cool spot for about forty-eight hours before cutting. When the soap has hardened up, take a spatula and lift the bars out one at a time and stack them up so that air can get to them for about two weeks. This is the amount of time it will take for the soap to "cure" and take some of the harshness out of it.

Hansford Hite on his seventy-fifth birthday

6

Hansford Clinton Hite

Vesuvius, Virginia

I'm not sure when I first met Hansford Hite and his wife, Dot, because, like so many of the mountain people, once you've met them, it's as if you've known them your whole life. I remember one instance when my mother was visiting from Florida, and I took her with me to the Hite farm to interview Hansford about the Narrow Passage schoolhouse located on his property. By the time we wound our way down Route 56, the steep twisting road where Golden Ridge Farm sat nestled into the mountain, my mom was ready to head back to the Florida flatlands. Before we left, Hansford filled the back of my old Bronco with fresh-picked cantaloupes from his garden, and we enjoyed the sweet, succulent melons all week. This completely redeemed him in the eyes of my mother, who couldn't believe how generous and giving these mountain people were, despite the fact they chose to live on the side of a mountain.

At Hanford's seventy-fifth birthday party in 1995, the family asked if I would come and take a few pictures and put them in the October issue of *Backroads*. I thought it would be more appropriate to write an interview, to go along with the photos, about a man who is well respected and much loved by everyone who has met him.

A tall man in stature, Hansford surprises you with his soft voice and gentle nature. Sitting in their home for the interview, the humorous banter and loving gestures between he and Dot indicated what a happy marriage they've had for fifty-five years.

Born to Viola Humphries and Emmett Hansford Hite on September 12, 1920, Hansford grew up on an idyllic hillside farm on South Mountain with his brother Norman and sisters Mary and Margaret. It was the very same farm that his great-great-grandfather, George Hite, had bought in the 1700s. A deed found in the Rockingham County courthouse states that George acquired 1,140 acres through a land auction, and eight generations of the Hite family have lived there ever since.

George also gave the land for South Mountain Chapel, also known as Haines Chapel, to be built on, and he was the first person to be buried in the church cemetery. Hansford's grandfather, Billy Hite, gave land to the Rockbridge County school system for a one-room schoolhouse; it was built on his farm property to educate the mountain children. The school, named Narrow Passage because of the narrow, boulder-lined lane into the farm, taught grades one through seven. Hansford attended the school, and he

Courtesy of Carol H. Harlow

Hansford and his siblings. From left: Hansford, Mary Edna, Margaret, Norman.

remembers his first teacher as being Flossie Fisher, who, like many of the teachers who taught there, boarded with his parents during the school term. Narrow Passage School is now owned by one of Hanford's sisters.

Hansford was living at home when at nineteen years of age he went to work on the Blue Ridge Parkway as a right-of-way cutter, working with crude tools such as cross-cut saws and brush axes. He said that the government advertised the jobs in the newspapers, since the mountain road they would be constructing would cover three counties in ten miles. He had to go to the employment office in Buena Vista for a Rockbridge County work card and then report for work on the mountain with about four hundred other men to vie for the coveted jobs. "I was real lucky because, in that the first day, they hired anybody up there, so I got picked," said Hansford.

He remembers they had an unusual system for picking the workers. Everyone would stand around in small groups and the job supervisor would point to a person. Each man in that particular group would slowly raise their hand until the one that was to be picked raised his, and the foreman would nod yes.

Their job for the next two years was to construct a ten-mile road from the top of the mountain at Route 56, north to Love Gap to a little sag just beyond Route 814.

Hansford met Dot for the first time just prior to his Parkway employment, while he was working in the apple orchards. Dot's older sister, Elsie, worked with Hansford. One Saturday evening, Dot and her current boyfriend came to pick up Elsie. Hansford said he kept sneaking looks at Dot out of the corner of his eye and was instantly attracted to the dark-haired, fifteen-year-old beauty, despite her boyfriend. His chance came later when his first cousin, who was then courting Elsie, became ill, and Hansford's family went to visit him. Who was there but Dot. "This time," said Hansford, "I could see her real good, without her knowing I was staring at her. I thought to myself, little girl, I just might fall in love with you!" A short time later, the cousin got better, resumed his courting, and Hansford asked him to put in a good word for him concerning Dot. Apparently Dot had done a fair amount of noticing the tall, handsome young man herself, and she accepted his offer to see her.

The rest, as they say, is history. On September 12, 1940, Hansford's twentieth birthday, he and Dot were married at two o'clock in the afternoon at the Vesuvius

Hansford and Dot on their wedding day, September 12, 1940

Baptist Church parsonage by Rev. D. M. McGrady. Dot was eighteen years old at the time, and her thoughtful groom had already seen to it that the vacant Narrow Passage schoolhouse was turned into a furnished, three-room bungalow—there they set up housekeeping.

To get three days off for his wedding, Hansford told his Parkway supervisor that he needed time off to dig the potatoes out of his garden, fearing if he told him the real reason, permission would be denied. Word leaked out about him "digging potatoes," and he took a fair amount of ribbing when he reported in for work the following Monday.

The crew of men worked their right-of-way up to Bald Mountain, then a dozer came behind them, clearing a rough roadway for the tons of gravel that had to be laid for the road base. Rock crushers were set up, and men from every farm in the vicinity would bring load after load of mountain rocks to be crushed and turned into gravel for the project. Hansford's take-home pay at this time was $11.88 weekly, which equaled 30¢ an hour for forty hours a week, minus the small change taken out for Social Security and taxes. Then Hansford changed jobs to dump-truck driver and his pay escalated to $17.82 a week, a jump to 45¢ an hour for forty hours. He said that he and Dot thought they were in high cotton with the extra money coming in. Over a period of time, however, that particular job finished, and Hansford went to work at Wayne Manufacturing in Waynesboro, working a grand total of six weeks before coming back home and cutting pulpwood for a living that winter.

Rumor had it that the next ten-mile phase of the Blue Ridge Parkway from Route 56 to Irish Gap was to begin that spring, so the young couple began hoping that Hansford would be able to get Parkway employment again. Other men seeking employment on the same job began asking about renting the old schoolhouse, so Hansford and Dot moved into the upstairs of his parent's home and made their own cozy apartment there until he finally did get a job on the Route 56 to Irish Gap roadway.

Two children (Wayne and Carol) were born while the Hites

were living there. When Hansford's parents gave him and Dot fourteen acres of their own in 1941, they started construction on a house; in 1942, they moved in. Their last two children (Doug and Jay) were born in that home. They called their place Golden Ridge Farm, and it continues to be called that today, even though the Hites sold their portion of the farm in 1991 when they decided to move down the mountain to be a little closer to the village of Vesuvius.

Over the years, Hansford continued working in road construction, then ended up retiring from Charles Barger and Son Company in Lexington, Virginia, where he had been the service manager of International, a truck dealership there. In latter years, Dot worked at the Whetstone Ridge Restaurant at milepost 29 on the Blue Ridge Parkway, White's Truck Stop, Sugar Tree Lodge, and Osceola Mill Bed-and-Breakfast.

The Hite family

Now that the Hites are both retired, I asked what they liked to do in their spare time. Dot makes old-fashioned cloth dolls, and Hansford enjoys making walking sticks and just puttering around. They enjoy their family and like to take short day trips. Both are active in the Montebello Senior Center and love to drive out to

Manley Allen and Bruce Clark's for the Tuesday and Friday evening music get-togethers. Hansford laughs good naturedly and says that the most fun they've had since retiring is arguing with one another.

Visiting with this couple in their beautiful home and listening to their happy chatter makes one realize that good marriages are still around. They have had their share of sadness, but they've emerged stronger because of their sorrows. It's plain that they dearly love each other and their family members. It was a real joy to sit down and talk with them both, and I thank Hansford and Dot Hite for making the November 1995 issue of *Backroads* a very special one.

Boyd Coffey, Reed's Gap, Virginia

The Pattersons boiling pon hoss in Sherando

7

Boiling Down "Pon Hoss"

Maynard Patterson, Sherando, Virginia

When the January 2001 issue of *Backroads* came out, there was an overwhelming positive response to the article about hog butchering, since so many people remember butchering day from their youth. As stated, hogs were the main meat staple on every mountain farmstead because families depended on every part of the animal to carry them through the lean winter months. From sausages and tenderloins to lard and lye soap, the hogs provided it all. Another tasty by-product from the animal during butchering time was what folk called "pon hoss," which was made from leftover scrap meat and cornmeal that are boiled down together. It was fried up crisp for breakfast or could be eaten at other meals or in between. Maynard Patterson and his family continue the practice and were kind enough to let me take photos of the process to publish in the March 2001 *Backroads*. Along with the pictures, I came home with several "loafs" of delicious pon hoss. Here's how the family makes it.

First off, I know that I am spelling pon hoss incorrectly. The general consensus was that the name is of Dutch or German origin. Since I am 100 percent Wiener Schnitzel, I looked through all my mother's German and Pennsylvania Dutch cookbooks but could not find any mention of it. There was plenty about souse, liver pudding, and pickled pigs feet but nothing on pon hoss. Someone said that the spelling could be "pan haus," but, again, even with that German spelling, I found nothing remotely similar. I have since learned from the Internet that it is actually "pon haus" and is Pennsylvania Dutch in origin, but I will continue to spell it as it's pronounced here in the Blue Ridge Mountains.

The first step in making pon hoss is to remove the eyes and inner ear parts on the hog's head before putting the head in a large cast iron kettle to boil. Many times, the whole head was saved from butchering day and frozen until needed. Other meat, such as the heart, liver, ears, and tongues were also added to the pot. The meat is kept at a steady boil until the meat comes off the bone. When it's finished cooking, the various parts are put into an old-fashioned hand-cranked grinder which Maynard and his son Dickie had rigged up with an electric motor. This makes for quicker grinding. The result is called "pudding meat." Everyone standing around got to taste the various meat products before they were ground up. I know anyone who hasn't tasted boiled tongue dipped in salt will make a face, but I am telling you, it is absolute ambrosia to the palate. Maybe it's my German background, but any kind of meat, fat, or by-product thereof has my vote.

When all the meat has been ground, the broth is then sieved, separating it from the stray bits of meat and bones still in the kettle. The broth is once again brought to a boil while about ten to twelve pounds of white cornmeal is mixed with water in large pans, making a soupy concoction. When the broth is sufficiently boiling, about one third of the pudding meat is added to the kettle, along with all the cornmeal. The mixture continues to boil and is ready when it starts to pull away from the sides of the kettle. The other two thirds of the pudding meat is packed into pans; this is known as "liver pudding." Once again, if you've never eaten it, you don't know what you're missing!

Once the pon hoss has thickened, it is seasoned, and the kettle is taken off the fire. The mixture is then ladled into containers. Maynard and his family save all sizes of throwaway aluminum pans throughout the year so no one has to keep up with where all the containers have gotten off to. That way, he can share pon hoss with family and friends without any fuss. The pon hoss sets up in

Checking to see if the meat is cooked

Grinding the pudding meat

Adding the pudding meat to the broth

Filling pans with the completed pon hoss

the pans and is then put in a cool place. Maynard's wife Kitty says it can also be frozen successfully until needed. About the only drawback to pon hoss is its likelihood to come apart when being fried. But hey, intact or crumbled, when something that good is fried up, you eat it any way it comes.

There are endless varieties of dishes that can be made from one simple hog. Souse is a gelatin dish made from the meat of the pig's feet and ears. And speaking of feet . . . ever try pickled pig's feet with a stack of soda crackers? Yum, yum. Scrapple is made from boiling cornmeal and broth together, minus the meat. So you see, this is why the hog was the most important animal in the mountain people's barnyard, foodwise.

Dickie Patterson exhibiting some mountain humor

I had a great time the day the men got together and made pon hoss. Their good-natured bantering and teasing had me in stitches all morning. Whenever you are around Maynard, you have to be prepared for plenty of ribbing. Before I took off for home, we did a fair amount of bartering. I promised to give Maynard an entire set of the photos that I had taken that day, plenty of extra *Backroads* to hand out, plus the notoriety of being in such a renowned newspaper! In return, I got fresh sausage, cracklins', a can of lard, and a huge pan of pon hoss. Everyone was a winner!

The Dodd's cabin, Beech Grove, Virginia

The bell tower at Mountain Top Church in Love, Virginia

8

Mountain Churches

Mountain Top, Haines Chapel, Mount Paran, and Evergreen

In the first volume of *Backroads*, I featured many of the early mountain schools located in our area of the Blue Ridge Mountains. In this second book, I'm presenting the histories of four old churches that have been serving God for countless years in the same areas. These churches were the very hub of the mountain people's lives, and they provided not only a place to worship but also a place to socially connect, since many folks lived in isolated hollows and didn't see anyone but their own families for weeks at a time. These were the days before everyone had cars and trucks, and they walked out of the hills to attend church.

The services usually ran from early spring to late fall, and preachers on horseback would ride a circuit, sharing the pastoring responsibilities for several churches, holding services at each church on different Sundays of the month or at different times on a single Sunday. Because of their circular trip around the mountains to each church, they were called "circuit riders." During the severe winter months, many times services would be suspended because the preachers could not make their rounds in the deep snow.

Here in the mountains, there is a tree called the "Service Berry" that is the first to bloom in the springtime. It got its name because when the white flowers of the tree blossomed, the people would know it was time for Sunday services to commence for the year. Come with me now on a trip back in time, when the pews in these little mountain churches were filled with people from the communities of Love, Montebello, Nash, and Rockbridge County, Virginia.

MOUNTAIN TOP CHRISTIAN CHURCH
Love, Virginia

Mountain Top Christian Church is located in Love, Virginia, at the top of the mountain where the Blue Ridge Parkway intersects with Route 814. It is now that community's only place of worship. The present building was built in 1921, but the original Mountain Top was located across the Parkway and down Campbell's Mountain Road apiece. The exact year that it was built is unknown, but, according to old records from Evergreen Christian Church (built in 1830), the church at Love, then known as Meadow Mountain, was a mission point for Evergreen. In 1884, a division was made, and Meadow Mountain became a church in itself.

Mountain Top Christian Church in the 1980s

I remember talking with Johnny Coffey about the old log church (later referred to as Mountain Top), and he told me it was a one-room log building, surrounded by huge oak trees that had wooden tables built between them that held the food for the annual homecoming and revival services. He also said there were hitching posts near the church for those riding horses instead of walking. The old sanctuary had coal oil lamps with silver reflectors to illuminate the church, since this was before electricity had come to the mountain. Johnny, whose family lived in Chicken Holler, recounts a few of his memories of attending the log church when he was just a young child.

We would usually walk to church on Sunday or else take the wagon. I used to wear little bib overalls and no shoes on my feet. My father and a lot of the other men from the area rode horse and wagons down Campbell's Mountain to the sawmill run by Mr. Cab Hatter where they bought lumber to make the pews. They hauled the wood back over that steep grade, and each family was responsible for making their own pew. When they were finished, they carved their last name in each bench, and that's where they would sit every Sunday. The people were poor, but they always supported their own church, seeing to it that it was well taken care of.

The Sunday school only ran from spring to fall, and whenever they were getting ready to close it for the winter months, a huge picnic was always planned. We used to have powerful "night meetings" [revivals] that were held in August of each year. There were usually a lot of folks who came each night, and the meetings ran a week long. Sometimes they would have an exceptionally good preacher, and the meetings would carry over for an extra week. People would come from miles around in their horse-drawn wagons just to hear the likes of Preacher Rice speak. He was one that could hold 'em on the edge of their pews! I can still see the lanterns glowing whenever the people left for home after the meetings were over.

Also held in August was our yearly reunion or homecoming service. Sometimes as many as three hundred people would come back to their home church for preaching, singing, and the old-fashioned dinner on the grounds held under those large oak trees. Why, Son, I've never seen such food as what they'd have at those reunions.

Johnny Coffey also told me about the baptisms they had at Mountain Top. He said there were three places they used: one was over in Chicken Holler near his brother Forest's

A homecoming dinner on the grounds of Mountain Top Church

house where there was a deep creek; another was down Route 814 across from Frank Hatter's house; and the last was below the old Saunder's camp where a deep pool of water was located. Anyone who has ever dipped their foot into the cold, clear water of Back Creek in the summertime will appreciate the hearty souls who went all the way under during the winter months. My husband, Billy, recalled stories of the preacher H. D. Coffey breaking the ice in order to baptize folks in the spring-fed mountain streams.

Sometime around 1920, the old church had fallen into disrepair. It was decided to build a new church closer to the graveyard at the top of the mountain at Love. The men started in on it and had the skeleton frame of the building erected when a big storm came up and blew the structure over. When they started over, the new church was moved farther up the hill from the graveyard.

Mr. John Will Everitt and his wife, Minnie, donated the land for the church. Henry Davis Coffey was the preacher who started Mountain Top, and he was also responsible for starting a lot of the other Christian Churches in the area, such as White Rock and Evergreen.

The first service was held in the new sanctuary in 1921, and H. D. Coffey preached the first sermon there. The log church from across the mountain was later torn down. Many of the families took their pews home when they dismantled the original church. Johnny said that he had his father's handmade pew for many years before it got so old it just fell apart.

Some of the early preachers who served Mountain Top Christian Church were Reilly Fitzgerald, Hoy Leake, "Preacher Boyd," John McKenney, "Preacher Perry," and Pettit Coffey, my husband's uncle, who held revivals there.

Mountain Top Church as it looks today

Currently, the little white church still holds Sunday school and worship services each week with about thirty people attending. Mountain Top has had several additions over the years, including a new vestibule, a large kitchen/Sunday school room, and an indoor bathroom, although they still have two wooden privies that are used during homecoming services. There are only a handful of ladies still attending whose parents and grandparents founded Mountain Top Christian Church. But those ladies are as faithful to come each Sunday as were their early relatives.

A quiet walk through the old graveyard tells a rich history of the area pioneers who made this small mountain community a very special place to live. This story is a written tribute to those fine people who carved out a living here in Love, Virginia, and worshipped their God at Mountain Top Christian Church throughout the years.

HAINES CHAPEL*
Rockbridge County, Virginia

One of the most picturesque mountain churches in our area, Haines Chapel (also known as South Mountain Chapel) has a rich and interesting history. Although the church no longer holds regular Sunday services, the white clapboard sanctuary is still used for the annual homecoming service, an Easter sunrise service, funeral services, and many weddings. In fact, my husband, Billy, and I chose to elope and exchange our wedding vows standing on the front porch of the chapel back in 1993.

Sitting high on a knoll overlooking South Mountain, Haines Chapel is the perfect spot for a private wedding because it is well off the main road, tucked away in the Virginia hills with breathtaking views of the surrounding countryside. The chapel has no electricity, which makes the Easter sunrise service even more meaningful for those attending. Each Easter while driving back on the winding road leading to the chapel, I see the soft yellow glow of coal oil lamps illuminating the church in the early morning darkness and am reminded that I am seeing the same sight our mountain forefathers saw almost two hundred years ago.

George Hite (sometimes spelled "Hight") was born on July 3, 1755, in King and Queen County, Virginia. In 1776, he moved with his father to Botetourt County. While there, he volunteered and served as a private in Captain Gilmore's Company, Colonel Christian's Virginia Regiment, on an expedition against the Cherokee Indian nation.

On August 14, 1777, he volunteered as a private in Captain Caswallader Jones's Troop, Col. George Baylor's Third Regiment

---

*Parts of this story were taken from A *History of Methodism in Rockbridge County, Virginia*, by Albert Cupp.

Haines Chapel as it looks now

of Light Dragoon. At the battle at Monks Corner, he, along with fifteen others, was captured and confined on board a prison ship until August 1781. After a prisoner exchange, he went to Jamestown, where he rejoined his regiment and served until discharged in the fall of 1782. He spent the remainder of his life on his farm, which he bought near Montebello in Rockbridge County, Virginia. George Hite married Lovis Lunsford and raised nine children: five boys and four girls.

On August 5, 1835, George Hite, wishing to make a much-needed religious contribution to his community, donated two and a half acres of land to the trustees of the Methodist/Episcopal church. The trustees were James Cash, Howell G. Humphries, John Kiger, John Albright, George Hite, David Shewey, and Frederick Allbright. The land was located near the top of the eastern slope of South Mountain in the eastern corner of Rockbridge County and was to be used for a church site and graveyard. The first church erected there was built from logs from the surrounding forest. George died on August 21, 1837, and was buried in the new graveyard under a large tree. The Virginia Historical Society placed a marker over his grave a few years back.

*George Hite's (Hight's) gravestone
in the Haines Chapel cemetery*

South Mountain Chapel was first on the Lexington circuit, and, according to a report, the preacher's salary for the conference year of 1835 was $3.50. In 1837, they paid $28.56 to Rev. John C. Lynn, preacher in charge.

The Fairfield circuit was formed in 1849, which then included South Mountain, Emory Chapel, and White's Gap.

South Mountain, with George Hite as its leader, cast its lot with the Northern branch of the church and did a good work for many years. As George Hite, along with all the other elderly members, passed on to their heavenly reward, the church was neglected for the want of a leader as well as a preacher.

About the year 1870, the Southern branch of the Methodist/Episcopal Church built a small frame church on the south side of the road, on top of the mountain where the road forks

The interior of Haines Chapel

to the Irish Creek Road. This church thrived for many years under the leadership of Robert S. Hite, a local preacher and the great-grandson of George Hite.

In 1915, the old South Mountain Chapel was rebuilt, and the name was changed to Haines Chapel. This chapel thrived for some years and had an active Sunday school, but by 1955, the only use the church had was for funeral services for those wishing to be buried there.

As stated above, Haines Chapel is now used for weddings, yearly homecoming and Easter sunrise services, as well as funerals. Several years ago, the church's exterior weatherboard was covered with vinyl siding to protect the chapel from exposure to the elements, a new wooden fence was built, and a picnic pavilion was added—all from donated money. The chapel continues to draw many visitors and family members whose loved ones are buried in the church graveyard.

MOUNT PARAN BAPTIST CHURCH
Montebello, Virginia

My husband, Billy, is the current pastor at Mount Paran. The church is special to us in that this is where Billy first started his ministry in the fall of 1999. The mountain church, sitting high on a hill overlooking the countryside, with cows grazing in the distance, has seen many changes since its beginning in 1869. This brief history, written in August 1982 by Rev. Virgil Pugh, pastor at that time, gives insight into the changes Mount Paran has undergone in its 141 years.

On October 1, 1869, in a building on the old Montebello Farm, local persons led in this faith met to organize the Mount Paran Baptist Church. The following founders and brethren were elected to office: pastor and moderator, Rev. J. C. Richardson; clerk and deacon, H. R. Fitzgerald; deacons, R. C. Grant, George Wood, John M. Grant, Preston Fitzgerald, John H. Painter, James A. Robertson, and Daniel S. Cash.

On October 24, 1892, as stated in the records of Nelson County, Virginia, E. J. and Mary S. Robertson deeded a parcel of land to the church. The trustees receiving this were James W. Hamilton, McDowell Fitzgerald, George B. Christ, E. D. Robertson, John C. Grant, and Peter J. Hite.

Pastors who served the church from 1869 until 1928 were as follows: Rev. J. C. Richardson, 1869–1870; Rev. S. P. Massie, 1870–1879; Rev. R. E. Gleason, 1875–1895; no permanent pastor from 1895–1897; Rev. S. P. Massie 1897–1907; no permanent pastor from 1907–1909; Rev. Paulis Massie, 1909–1918; Rev. A. R. Crabtree, 1918–1919; no permanent pastor from 1919–1921; Rev. R. M. Taylor, 1921–1925; no permanent pastor from 1925–1927; Rev. J. F. Murray, 1927–1928. There was preaching on the third Sunday to this date.

On January 30, 1907, a deed was made by Rosa and James W. Bartley, conveyed to trustees McDowell Fitzgerald, D. M. Cash, S. P. Grant, George Cash, and Nelson Grant, to enlarge the grounds to accommodate a cemetery, and an addition was granted by same in 1943 to trustees G. V. Cash, A. M. Fitzgerald, and E. D. Robertson.

In July 1918, A. R. Crabtree was called to preach at Mount Paran. He was the first pastor to live in the parsonage of the Montebello Church. This home was located on the right-hand side of the Painter Mountain Road, just beyond and joining the Montebello High School grounds, Route 56, east of the Montebello Post Office. He lived there until he left in October 1919.

Rev. Paulis Massie, who served
as pastor from 1909 to 1918

Rev. William Rodney Vaiden pastored the church from 1931 until 1935. Under his leadership, the church replaced the one-room structure that had served the congregation up to this time. As a supply pastor, L. G. Humphries served the church from 1935 until E. M. Ramsey accepted a call to this field in 1936. He was succeeded by Rev. D. N. McGrady in December 1937 and served until 1943.

Construction of the new sanctuary in the 1930s

Both churches at Mount Paran before the old church was dismantled

Rev. Jesse E. Tate served from 1943 until 1947. Student Pastor Daniel Spell served from 1947 until 1951. Rev. Charles S. Bateman served from 1947 until 1954. Rev. Richard Calhoun came in 1954 and served until 1965. Rev. U. W. Giles came in 1965 and served until 1967. The first fulltime pastor was Charles E. Williams, who arrived in 1968 and served until 1975. Claude L. Crawford served as a supply preacher during the times when the church was without a permanent pastor.

The church built a new parsonage in 1954. Trustees for the new parsonage were Merlin Grant, Paulus Fitzgerald, and Nevel Seaman. Land was given by Leslie and C. C. Robertson, with water rights from A. H. and Allie Bradley.

Mount Paran would not forget to be very thankful for the late Rev. Scott C. Hutton on whom the congregation could always depend. It was Rev. Hutton who brought Virgil Pugh to Mount Paran on June 22, 1975, to a birthday dinner of the beloved Mrs. Lottie Anderson. On August 31 of that same year, Virgil Pugh preached his first sermon at Mount Paran and was called to be their fulltime pastor. He and his wife, Daisy, moved to Montebello on January 26, 1976. Virgil, beloved pastor at Mount Paran, died suddenly while digging ginseng in the mountains in September 1982. The church later called Dan Naude of South Africa to serve in Virgil's place from 1983 to 1986.

Rev. Dave Anderson served from 1987 to 1989; Rev. Jim Simmons from 1989 to 1991; Rev. Stan Middleton began his ministry in 1992 but became ill and was out for a time recovering. Rev. Stan Fann filled the pulpit until Stan Middleton was well enough to return. Rev. Middleton then served until 1998. Rodney Zirkle served from 1998 to 1999; Rev. Billy Coffey served from November 1999 until December 2002; Rev. Wyatt Mays from 2003 until 2007. The current pastor, Billy Coffey, returned to Mount Paran in November 2007 and continues to serve at this time [2010].

The first church building served the Mt. Paran congregation for forty-two years before construction of a new sanctuary began in 1933. The old sanctuary was taken down when the church moved into the new building in 1934. The present building has under-

The Mount Paran Baptist Church in Montebello, Virginia

gone several changes in the last seventy-six years. The old weatherboard siding was overlaid with brick in the 1950s. During the years 2008–2009, Buddy and Jacob Waymack and Ray Shipman built a new addition onto the front of the church. Danny Barker, member and deacon at Mt. Paran at that time, laid the brick for the new addition. The addition housed a handicapped bathroom as well as a nursery for the babies of the congregation.

It was also discovered that the original bricks covering the back of the church were crumbling and needed replacing, so Danny Barker was enlisted to replace them after the new addition was finished. A large picnic pavilion was built and used for the annual church homecoming service, held on the third Sunday in August, as well as other events. The new pavilion was dedicated on October 8, 2005, to Homer Anderson and his wife, Louise, whose property adjoins the church and who generously donated the land where the pavilion was built.

The beautiful church, surrounded by stately oak trees, has served God and the Montebello community well during its long history and still holds weekly Sunday services for those wishing to attend.

EVERGREEN CHRISTIAN CHURCH*
Nash, Virginia

Perhaps the oldest Christian Church in our area is Evergreen Christian Church in Nelson County, Virginia, located along the North Fork of the Tye River at Nash. A disciple minister named Joshua Webb came into the area to preach in the 1830s. Jackson Darst, author of *Ante-Bellum Virginia Disciples*, writes of Webb: "Joshua Webb of Augusta, an almost ephemeral character who emerges long enough to establish this work and then disappears." In any case, Henry B. Coffey was one of his converts, and he subsequently became one of our ministers in Nelson County. Mr. Coffey was ordained by the church as a pastor on July 10, 1838. He was licensed by the court to celebrate marriages on October 24, 1842.

According to old records, an acre and a half was deeded to the Disciples of Christ and the Baptist faiths by Andrew J. and Rebecca Campbell, who gave the land for a church to be built upon. Although the exact date of the deed is not known, it suggests that the new church was to be shared by the two faiths, worshipping in the building at different times.

The old Evergreen Christian Church

H. Davis Coffey, who was instrumental in starting a number of Christian Churches in Virginia, as well as specifically in our area, was Henry B. Coffey's grandson. One old record of a board meeting is dated December 29, 1883. It states: "The church was named 'Evergreen' at this meeting." The important thing is that Henry Coffey seems to have been the founder of this church.

Aubrey J. Coffey, a kinsman of Henry B. Coffey writes: "His ordination certificate states: 'This is to certify to all who it may concern that our beloved Henry B. Coffey has been legally ordained a preacher of the Gospel of Christ on Tye River. And as such we recommend him to wherever God and His providence may cast his lot.

---

*Information for this story came from the books *My Life with God: New Sermons*, by H. D. Coffey, and *History of Evergreen Christian Church*, by A. J. Coffey.

Henry B. Coffey

Henry Davis Coffey

Given under our hands this the 10th day of July 1838. Signed Elder Joshua Webb, Elder B. H. Kindez, and Elder Edmund Coffey.'"

In the early days of this congregation, worship was many times held out of doors. The first building used was probably the old log building that was torn down near the lower side of the present church house. It was made of hand-hewed logs. There was a sharp division among the people about where the building should be placed. There were some who wanted it where it was later placed, and others who wanted it at or near the South Fork of the Tye River. Division over the location became so intense, it is said that

The present Evergreen Christian Church

one group came in and cut all the logs in two. When a new set of logs were being hewed, a fight followed which drew blood, and one man was seriously injured. The building was used until the present building was erected; then the old log church was sold for $30.00.

As primitive as it might have been, some of our finest preachers used it: George W. Abell, Robert L. Coleman, Z. Parker Richardson, Frank Berry, Landon A. Cutler, E. R. Perry, and others. Some of our finest church people worshipped in it.

When he was not quite ten years of age, H. D. Coffey was converted in a meeting held in this old church by George W. Abell. J. Riley Fitzgerald, who lived on the North Fork of the Tye River, preached at Evergreen over a long period of time. The Campbells, Coffeys, and Fitzgeralds were leaders in this church. Brother A. J. Coffey says of Riley Fitzgerald that "he did most of his preaching at Mountain Top, White Rock, and Evergreen."

H. D. Coffey was one of the pastors at Evergreen Church. He also taught school in the old church house. H. D. writes:

> Old Evergreen was built of logs, some of which were eighteen inches wide, and stood without finishing for several years. Then we decided to put in a good floor, ceil the building, and put in windows and good doors. I worked in this about seven weeks and then taught school in it. It was there I was ordained by Bro. E. R. Perry and there that I tried to preach my first sermon. We had fine Sunday Schools there for several years.

In 1870, Henry B. Coffey was pastor, and George W. Abell, a state evangelist, came to hold a meeting. In his report to the State Missionary Board on October 1870, Brother Abell writes:

> At Arrington Station, left the cars and, in company with a Brother Campbell [brother of H. D.'s mother] and son of Brother Coffey [B. F., uncle of H. D.], proceeded on my way to the house of the latter, some twenty miles from Arrington, near the headwaters of the Tye River, the scene of my next appointment. This was a romantic and picturesque little trip, the pure limpid waters gliding over smooth

stones and golden sands, leaping over gentle cataracts, murmuring praises to their Creator in the ears of magnificent hills and mountains, standing in breathless, silent attention; these pure waters reminding one of the waters of life, as they gushed from the throne of God, in primeval days, ere the foul feet of tradition had polluted them.

I was fully repaid and refreshed on arriving at the cottage of Brother Coffey, in this sequestered and romantic portion of the world, and finding there the highest order of humanity, a Christian gentleman and a Christian family. Some twenty-five years ago, I had comforted them in committing two of their innocent lambs into the gentle arms of a kind Shepherd, and subsequently baptized two more, the one now a husband and father [H. D.'s father, Andrew J.], the other a wife and a mother, and the whole family in the kingdom of Christ.

The next day, commenced our meeting in these parts. The work commenced here where it seldom does, but always ought, right in the pulpit; the first person to confess the Lord being a preacher, a Mr. Fitzgerald from Kentucky, who thirty years ago, assumed Wesley for his leader and became a member of the Methodist Church, but upon the invitation being given, walked down out of the stand and took his seat as an humble confessor and upon making the good confession, was baptized in the name of the Lord Jesus, for the remission of his sins. . . . I gave him the solemn charge of Paul to Timothy, "preach the word."

This was the most interesting meeting I ever held. Up to Thursday, the fifth day, there were forty three confessions, ranging from nine [this was H. D.'s confession] to ninety years; the last day, there having been seven, when, in the midst of such interest, I was compelled to leave to fill other engagements.

Thursday night I spent under the roof of Brother Captain Fitzpatrick, Arrington Station.

This Captain Fitzpatrick is, no doubt, the one Dr. Jackson Darst relates:

Colonel Alexander Fitzpatrick (1799–1871), a wealthy attorney near Lovingston, was an independent thinker,

read the Bible for himself, and had unknowingly come to
the Disciples' position before he ever heard of the New
Testament brethren. In spite of having been told the slan-
der that the "Campbellites" simply "ask a man if he
believes Jesus is the Christ, and if he replies affirmatively,
they baptize him," he went to hear R. L. Coleman, who
had recently become a Disciple. After Coleman's dis-
course, Fitzpatrick declared to him, "That is the first
gospel sermon I ever heard. It is the first time the gospel
has ever been preached in Nelson County."

Brother Coffey writes that when he was seventy-seven years old:

About 1916, another church building was erected
adjoining the site of the original, being led by my cousin
Aubrey J. Coffey, now of Logan, West Virginia, but who at
that time was a student at Lynchburg College. He and I
were raised in that section. The men of the community
went to the mountains and cut the lumber and hauled it to
a sawmill and sawed the lumber for most of the building.
Some of the men gave almost two months' time to this
work. Money was raised for the necessary material to complete the church. The women of the community brought
basket dinners each day for the scores of men who were
working on the building. The building began on a Monday
morning and on the following Sunday, it was packed with
a happy congregation. I go back there to preach sometimes, but find that all the old leaders have died.

As serene as this church seemed in its location, with majestic
mountain peaks before it, a rising mountain behind it, and a musical stream flowing close by in front of it, no one would ever dream
of catastrophe and disaster coming suddenly on such a peaceful
scene, but it did! In August 1969, Hurricane Camille swept down
on Central Virginia during the night and morning hours of August
19 to 20. It hit Nelson County with such an amazing rainfall,
thirty-one inches to be exact, that floods sprang up through the
entire area. The raging waters carried houses, people, cars, bridges,
and boulders away. "Trees swept by like matchsticks," one survivor

related. Mudslides caused considerable damage. At least 125 lives were lost in Nelson County alone, many of the bodies were never found. The Evergreen Church was nearly destroyed by the raging stream nearby that had once been so placid.

Subsequently, members of the Lynchburg Area Christian Men's Fellows accepted the project to restore the building. For several weeks, when any of the men could go to Nelson County, they assisted in laying new foundations, putting in new floors, painting, installing a new furnace, and putting up new outbuildings. Christian churches in Virginia gave financial aid, and the church was put back in good order. The young people of National City Christian Church in Washington, DC, raised money to give the church a new piano and came down in a group one Sunday to make the presentation. The Hopewell Church donated a communion set.

Serenity restored—the Evergreen Church in winter

A rededication service was held on November 30, 1969. Many members from area churches were in attendance. The program was a combination of dedicating the restored building and licensing and commissioning the pastor.

Gavin Fitzgerald being baptized by Billy Coffey

9

River Baptizing

Our congregation at Mount Paran Baptist Church in Montebello, Virginia, still practices baptism by immersion, which is to say, the person being baptized is completely submerged under water. Our belief is taken directly from the Bible, where it tells of John baptizing Jesus in the River Jordan, and, down through the years, our faith continues to do it in that way.

Many churches have a built-in baptismal, usually behind and above the pulpit so that the congregation can have a clear view of those being baptized. Others have a portable baptismal that can be filled with water for the ceremony and then emptied after use. But the majority of the mountain people in the churches where my husband has preached want to be baptized in the river. This is a very holy ritual that the entire church body takes to heart and supports with their presence. Many times, there is the singing of hymns and scripture reading from the Bible before each candidate is asked to come into the water to be baptized by the preacher.

When my husband, Billy, was pastoring Cornerstone Baptist Church in Tyro, we used the Tye River, where Routes 56 and Campbells Mt. Road intersect at the bridge. There have also been baptizing behind Junior Allen's house and at Nash where the North and South Forks of the Tye River come together.

Pat Thompson being baptized by his
father-in-law, Billy Coffey, in summer 2003

At Mount Paran, we use the "deep hole" along the North Fork of the Tye River, just up from Evergreen Christian Church at Nash. During the hot summer months, the children of the community use the place as a swimming hole. There are ropes dangling from overhanging tree limbs that the kids swing out on before plunging into the cold, clear water of the Tye. This place has one of the prettiest settings for a baptism imaginable, and we use it year round. No one seems to mind being baptized in December, as well as August, and, to my knowledge, no candidate has ever gotten a cold after being immersed in the frigid waters during the winter months. Others have said that in the earlier years at Mount Paran, people were baptized in the Montebello Campground lake, as well as the creek near the Fish Hatchery and the deep pools along the South Fork of the Tye River.

At each church, the congregations have special places where baptism takes place. In the previous chapter on mountain churches, Johnny Coffey stated that there were three different spots that Mountain Top Christian Church used for baptisms: one in a deep creek near his

Preacher Billy Morris baptizing
Erby Loan in the Tye River

brother Forest's home in Chicken Holler, another down Route 814 across from Frank Hatter's homeplace in Back Creek, and still another below the old Saunders camp, also located on Route 814.

I've heard Margie Hatter many times refer to the "baptizing hole" farther up the North Fork of the Tye, just below the old Massie camp, as where the members of White Rock Church were immersed in years past. I never fail to look over to the spot whenever we ride our horses up North Fork Road and marvel at the beauty of that particular place. Huge boulders rise above the deep pool as water cascades down into it.

The Union Baptist Church in Avon baptized in the waters of Williams Creek, just a short way up from the church. My good friend Ted Hughes gave me a 1940s photo of the Union congregation baptizing in Williams Creek that was found in his mother's personal belongings after her death.

Baptizing in Williams Creek

I have a treasury of old photographs in which various churches here in the mountains were having a river baptism. The ones I was a part of were led by preacher Billy Morris, founder of Cornerstone Baptist Church in Tyro, as well as Rev. Jerry Hopkins, a later preacher at the same church. Rev. Stan Shirk, who was pastor at Mt. View Mennonite Church, baptized in Back Creek, which gently flowed by the church. In fact, I believe it was here that I first witnessed an outdoor water baptism, and it was his young daughter, Sandy, who requested it. After our own son-in-law, Pat Thompson, became a Christian, he wanted to follow Jesus' example of baptism. One misty August day in 2003, we all drove over to the deep hole on the North Fork where Billy had the privilege of lowering Pat under the clear waters of the Tye and watching him emerge a "new creature in Christ."

An early 1900s baptism for Mount Paran Baptist Church

Down through the ages, the holy ritual of baptism has been done many ways, but, here in the gentle mountains of the Blue Ridge, people continue to request it be done in the familiar rivers and creeks of home.

Martha Goode Coffey's cabin, Love, Virginia

Making sorghum in Clifford, Virginia

10

Sorghum

Nature's Sweetener

E ach fall, Clifford, Virginia, celebrates its annual sorghum festival. Clifford is located in Amherst County, just south of
Lowesville on Route 151, and the Clifford Ruritan Club
sponsors the event. Although the community of Clifford is not
large in size, there is nothing small about the festival, which has all
the fun of a country fair with booths offering everything from
antique tools and glassware to country music and a jousting tour-
nament. But what draws the crowds the most is watching the
process of boiling down the juice from raw sugar cane into a thick,
dark syrup.

Mr. Clyde Mawyer, who is a member of the Ruritan Club, was
kind enough to explain the method by which the sweetener called
sorghum (molasses) is obtained through a boiling-down process
called "pulling the molasses." Watching it firsthand made it easier
to understand, and the photographs capture each stage as it is happening.

The first step in molasses making is cutting the cane out of the
field and then stripping the blades and cutting the tops off. The
sugar cane used for this particular festival was grown on the old
Episcopal Glebe property in Amherst County. It is then brought to
the Ruritan grounds and fed into a two-horse sorghum mill, where
it is crushed or squeezed to extract the juice. In the days when
horses or mules powered the mill, it was set upright and the cane

was fed into the machine vertically. Now that the mill is motor-
ized, they've turned it horizontally to make it easier for the men to
feed the cane into the mill.

Juice being pumped into pans

Stoking the fire box

Skimming off the foam

The finished product

When the juice is extracted, it is pumped over to evaporator pans which have a fire built under them, and a sequence of boiling ("hard, not so hard, and easy") takes place until the molasses is the right consistency. They say you can tell when the sorghum is ready by the bubbles in the pans. The bubbles are measured as "bird's eye" and "calf's eye"; if they are as big as a calf's eye, the sorghum has been boiled too much.

The liquid must be continually skimmed with a flat skimmer tool, which takes away the impurities, until the sorghum is ready to be put into mason jars. Each stage of the boiling process is separated by a wooden gate until the final product is fed into the last evaporator pan and ready for canning. It is at this final stage that "pulling the molasses" comes to fruition and must be handled very quickly, much like making fudge.

While I took photos of the molasses boiling down, I was rewarded with a taste of the rich, dark syrup. As I licked the last of it off my fingers, I asked Clyde what sorghum was good with. Suggestions came from every person within earshot: cornbread, fresh biscuits, shoo-fly pie, candy, ginger snaps, baked beans, gingerbread, and virtually anything made with sugar can use sorghum as a substitute.

I picked up a pamphlet at the festival by the National Sweet Sorghum Producers. It had some great recipes and an explanation of what sorghum actually is. I found the article very informative and the recipes sound delicious.

WHAT IS SORGHUM?

Sorghum is made from 100 percent pure, natural juice extracted from sugar cane. The juice is cleansed of impurities and concentrated by evaporation in open pans into clear, dark-amber colored, mild-flavored syrup. The syrup retains all of its natural sugars and other nutrients. It contains no chemical additives of any kind.

Sorghum is one of the oldest natural sweeteners known. We do not know when man first made and used it, but we do know that when America was being settled, it was the "principal sweetnin'" used by the colonists. The sorghum-cooking pan traveled westward with the early pioneers and thus became a part of our country's heritage. Besides being the energy food of the settlers, it made their foods more tasty and nutritious. Sorghum contains many hard-to-find nutrients such as calcium, iron, potassium, and phosphorous.

The colonists found many ways to use sorghum in their daily lives. From sweetening drinks and making confections to flavoring meats and baking, sorghum was the number one choice by everyone. It was used in place of granulated sugar in making pies, cakes, breads, puddings, and cookies.

Today's nutrition-conscious homemakers are rediscovering the versatility of sorghum that was first enjoyed by the colonists. They are finding there is hardly a food served today that sorghum won't improve. The syrup blends beautifully with every kind of food, enhancing both taste and texture in subtle ways. For today's chef, sorghum is a nutritious flavoring, a seasoning ingredient, and a sugar substitute. It's that secret ingredient that gives any food the delicious taste and aroma that spells homemade!

SORGHUM RECIPES

Barbecue Sauce

1 medium onion, minced

¼ cup vinegar

¼ cup sorghum

¼ teaspoon chili powder

1 cup catsup

Sauté onion in a small amount of fat. Mix all ingredients together and simmer about ten minutes. Baste on meat as desired.

Gingerbread

1 cup sugar

1 cup shortening

2 eggs, well beaten

1 cup sorghum

½ teaspoon salt

1½ teaspoons baking soda

1 teaspoon ground ginger

1 teaspoon cinnamon

2½ cups sifted flour

1 cup hot water

Preheat oven to 350 degrees. Cream sugar and shortening. Add eggs and sorghum and beat well. Sift dry ingredients together, add to sorghum mixture, and stir well. Add hot water and mix. Pour into a greased 9 x 12-inch pan. Bake for fifteen minutes.

Indian Bread

1½ cups sifted whole-wheat flour

1 cup cornmeal

½ cup powdered milk

1 teaspoon baking soda

2 teaspoons salt

¼ cup sorghum

1¼ cups water

Combine flour, cornmeal, powdered milk, soda, and salt. Add sorghum and water. Mix only until blended. Pour into top of a 1.5-quart double boiler. Place over hot water; cover and cook about one and a half hours or until sharp knife inserted in center comes out clean. Add water as needed to bottom half of double boiler. Cool about five minutes before removing from pan.

Oven Caramel Corn

2 cups brown sugar

2 sticks butter or margarine

½ cup sorghum

½ teaspoon salt

1 teaspoon vanilla

½ teaspoon baking soda

pinch of cream of tartar

15 to 20 cups popped corn

2 cups peanuts (optional)

Preheat oven to 250 degrees. Combine brown sugar, butter, sorghum, and salt. Cook four minutes over medium heat. Stir in vanilla, soda, and cream of tartar. Pour immediately over popped corn and peanuts in a large bowl. Mix to coat all pieces. Transfer to shallow pan and bake for one hour. Stir every fifteen minutes. Cool and store in an airtight container.

Jake Hewitt's barn, Love, Virginia

Ron Richardson demonstrates the art of dowsing

11

Dowsing for Water

Ron Richardson, Waynesboro, Virginia

My daughter Heather worked for a neurologist and was always telling me about a man who came in for treatment for his MS. She said Ron Richardson was a unique man, interested in the same things that interested me, and he would make a great interview for *Backroads* newspaper. I took her up on her offer of introduction, and, sure enough, I found Ron to be an exceptionally talented man who not only let me interview him but also went on to write many informative articles in the paper for many years. Employed by the U.S. Forest Service before taking a medical retirement, Ron had vast knowledge of anything concerning the outdoors. He wrote stories about the great chestnut trees and their untimely demise, digging ginseng, harvesting all types of wild edibles, and "The Little Crow Chronicles," a monthly series of fictional stories about a young Indian boy and his adventures within his tribe. In the October 2002 issue of *Backroads*, he submitted an article about dowsing and came up to our cabin to give us a demonstration of how it worked. The following is the article that Ron wrote for *Backroads* and which I am honored to include in this book.

With a bad drought come poor crops, brown pasture fields, and wells going dry. And when a water supply is threatened, people often call on those skilled in finding a new supply in an old way. These folks are called "dowsers," and the only tool they need to locate water is a dowsing rod, which can be made from a forked tree branch or a metal coat hanger.

Some people claim to be able to use a dowsing rod to find a lost person, read people's minds, pick a winner in the stock market, or choose the best day to plant potatoes. It is no wonder that the art of dowsing is shrouded in mystery and confusion and many think it is a tool of the devil. The scientific community admits the existence of dowsing but does not believe it is accurate or reliable enough to be of any permanent value.

I think you will find dowsing an interesting and unusual subject, and I'd like to share some of my knowledge of dowsing based on thirty years of experience using it. During that time, I have used a bent wire to locate underground pipes, telephone cables, gas lines, etc. Being able to locate things of this nature was a very useful skill to me. I have always been very grateful to the man who first showed me how to dowse years ago.

The only time that dowsing has failed to work for me was the few years following a head injury. I have absolutely no idea why this was, but, even after my injury healed, I have not been as good a dowser as I once was.

I don't do much dowsing nowadays. You've got to do a good bit of walking in trying to locate a source of water, and my legs don't get me around near as good as they used to, so I limit my dowsing to showing interested people how I do it.

For those of you who would like to give dowsing a try, here's how I go about it. Maybe I'd better mention now that dowsing does not work for everyone. The only advice I can offer along those lines is to try it several times before you give up.

First, you'll need a dowsing rod. Since all my experience has been with metal rods, that is what I'll talk about here. I first straighten out a twenty- to twenty-eight-inch-long piece of wire coat hanger because there always seems to be one handy when I need it. Copper, brass, and steel seem to work the same, so whatever you have on hand should do. Bend the wire five inches at one end into a right angle to form a handle. You now have an L-shaped dowsing rod in just a few minutes that is ready to go to work. Now comes the fun part! Grip the handle just firmly enough so that the rod doesn't move around on its own. Keep the rod as level as possible and pointed straight ahead.

First-time dowsers Heather Ayers and her brother Mike Coffey

Pick a spot in your yard or field where you know the approximate location of an underground pipeline or an electric line. Since this is your first attempt, it is best to stay away from areas that are criss-crossed with such lines. Walk slowly along, keeping the rod level and pointed straight ahead. For me, as soon as I step across the underground object, the rod turns in my hand and points outward, away from the side of my body. With some people the rod may turn inward. Both results mean the same thing; you've found something that was hidden under the ground. It's a weird feeling the first time it happens, but, after a few thousand times, you get used to it.

You now have taken your first step in dowsing. Finding the spot to dig a well requires a good bit more training and experience that time doesn't permit today. I can't help you with the horseracing, mind reading, or planting your potatoes, either, since those things aren't in my bag of tricks.

I have not explained exactly how dowsing works for good reason. I don't know how it works, any more than I know how electricity or my color television works. I hope I have, however, provided some insight into an interesting and unusual phenomenon.

Wild ramps

12

Wild Edibles

Nettle Weed, Wild Asparagus, Ramps, and More

One of the most interesting and useful things I have ever learned here on the mountain was what edible plants were growing in the woods and fields near the hunting camp where we lived. I found that they were not only palatable but also quite delicious and packed with the natural vitamins and nutrients our bodies need—plus, they were free for the taking.

Bunny Stein introduced me to the book *Stalking the Wild Asparagus*, by Euell Gibbons, and I was hooked. I went on to buy more and more books about gathering and cooking wild plants and have made them a big part of my life in the succeeding years. Besides the delicious recipes I've fixed for my family, many of these plants can be used for medicinal purposes as well.

People simply don't realize how many helpful and delicious foodstuffs there are growing right outside their door, not just here in the mountains but close to town, too. Each season produces its own delights, and the Native American Indians and early settlers calculated each plant's specialty by the time of the year it grew.

For instance, coltsfoot, which is one of the very first tiny yellow flowers that appear here in early March, is an excellent medicine for coughs. The leaves can be boiled down for tea or for making cough drops that bring soothing relief to a sore throat. The Native Americans ate young spring dandelion leaves to purify the blood. In summer, common mullein leaves applied to the skin can relieve the pain of a sunburn, and spotted touch-me-lot leaves, when boiled into a "tea" and applied to the affected area, can reduce the itch of poison ivy.

Nettle weed, the same plant that brings instant stinging pain when brushed up against, is possibly the most succulent of all native greens growing in the Blue Ridge and is a powerhouse of vitamins. If you've never tasted wild asparagus, which grows abundantly along fencerows in the early spring, you're missing out on a real taste treat. Asparagus is very pricey in the supermarket, but the wild variety tastes better and is free if one is willing to go gather it. Morels are one of the most sought-after spring mushrooms here in the mountains, and people are as secretive about the "spots" where morels grow as they are about their "zang patches" (ginseng). There was so much about morel mushroom hunting in issues of *Backroads* newspaper over the years that I felt it deserved it's own space, so it, and the recipes that go with it, will appear in the next chapter.

This list is just a smidgeon of the many edible plants that grow locally, and why more people aren't taking advantage of their use is beyond me. I always tell people, there were no Safeway stores in the Garden of Eden, and God gave us what we needed for a balanced diet right under our noses. There aren't any additives, steroids, or preservatives to worry about, and each season gives us exactly what we need. A big plus in today's world with obesity problems is that to *obtain* the wild foods, we have to walk to them, thus getting our exercise while gathering free food. It's a win-win situation!

When I first moved to the tiny village of Love, Virginia, a few neighbors started having what we called "wild parties," which to some might sound like police intervention was needed; but no, ours was a tamer affair. They were actually covered-dish dinners in which all the food had to be made from plants and animals found in the wild. These parties were a tribute to creativity, as each person carefully planned what they would cook. Each dish was quite different, and it was fun sampling the variety of recipes folks thought up. There were no standard cookbook recipes to go by, so one had to fly by the seat of their pants in food preparation. That's what made it so much fun!

I remember the first wild party. Bunny and I made invitations from rolled-up birch bark; the information for the party was printed with the dark purple juice from elderberries. We figured that if everything was to be made from the wild, we might as well start with the invitations. Everyone responded with enthusiasm, and all looked forward to how it would turn out. That first party was held in the late fall, and we soon realized that there are different foodstuffs available at that time of year. Later, we had another wild party in the spring, and the menu changed drastically. The guest list included several middle-aged married couples, a few single folks, and some young married couples with small children. All of our wild parties were held at Boyd and Gladys Coffey's Quonset hut, located over on Reed's Gap Road.

As casserole dishes were unwrapped, we all oohed and ahhed over what everyone had brought. There were myriad meats, vegetables, breads, and desserts to look over and sample. I remember that it was the first time I had ever tasted groundhog and was amazed at how good it was. Gladys Coffey had prepared the young "whistle pig" with potatoes and carrots, and you couldn't tell it from beef roast. Bunny made acorn muffins from meal she had ground from the nuts and leached with water to get the bitter tannin out. They had an earthy, nutty flavor that tasted heavenly. Rockwell and Ruby Harris made a blackberry cobbler from berries they had harvested during the summer and frozen, as well as some mighty fine sweet wine from the same batch. I cooked a big fat grouse (complete with stuffing) that had flown into the glass door on our back porch the day before the party. I remember thinking how much I appreciated his untimely death! Boyd Coffey added another first to my wild game repertoire by fixing bear meat. I've been sold on it ever since and cannot for the life of me understand people who say the meat is tough. See chapter 24 on wild game recipes for a foolproof way to prepare bear that will leave your mouth watering for more.

The spring wild party took a different turn as the season blessed us with a whole new set of foods. Buddy Stein picked morel mushrooms and made fabulous mushroom bisque. My daughter Heather and I made a salad out of crawdads and the watercress that grew by our spring. We had the fun of fishing for crawdads along Back Creek, then bringing them home to boil. They taste just like the lobster you get in a fancy restaurant, only smaller.

One of the funniest incidents at a wild party was when we invited William and Becky Hatter (newly arrived from Richmond). Becky said that she didn't know how to gather and cook food that didn't come from a store. We told her that was the one prerequisite for attending this type of dinner party. She surprised everyone with a wild rice recipe that was truly delicious. When asked about the dish, she smugly replied that it was a recipe her "Uncle Ben" had given her. We all had a good laugh, and, after that, everyone tried to cut her some slack.

The "wild parties" of Love, Virginia, went on for several years, with folks trying the new and different foods that God has provided man since the beginning of life on earth. Everything we need is before us if we but take the time to gather it. The Indians knew all about these foods because they were all that stood between starvation and survival. We have gotten used to the convenience of going to the store and buying frozen meals that we know are not as healthy for us and cost an arm and a leg. But the real food is still out there, waiting. Winter, spring, summer, and fall—the four seasons yield their bounty to anyone willing to partake. Maybe this will be the year you buy a wild edible book and see for yourself. Happy foraging!

To help you get going, here are a few recipes that are easy to prepare after you've gathered the wild foodstuffs and brought them home.

PERSIMMON-HICKORY NUT BREAD

I found this recipe in the early 1980s, and everyone who has ever eaten this dark-brown, moist sweet bread always asks for more. Persimmons (also known as sugar plums) are ready for harvest in the late fall, usually after a good frost. If you locate a wild persimmon tree, you can go back year after year to gather what you need. You've got to be quick about it, though, because possums, raccoons, and deer love the sweet fruit, too.

One good thing is that you don't need much of the pulp to make two nice-sized loaves. The years during which hickory nuts are sparse, you can substitute pecans, walnuts, or black walnuts. To render down persimmons into pulp I use my mother's old aluminum food mill with its wooden handle, but a hand-cranked food mill will work fine, too. Just make sure the persimmons are very ripe or else your mouth will turn "inside-out" with the alum taste. When the orange fruit is soft and mushy and has fallen to the ground, it's a sure bet that they are ready. Okay, here's what you'll need and how to make it:

2 cups flour

1 teaspoon baking soda

1 cup sugar

1½ sticks butter

2 eggs, well beaten

1 cup persimmon pulp

½ cup hickory nuts (or other nutmeats)

Preheat oven to 325 degrees. Sift flour and baking soda together. In a separate bowl, cream sugar and butter. Add eggs and stir. Mix slowly with the flour/soda mixture. Add persimmon pulp and nuts, and stir into a stiff batter. Pour into a well-greased loaf pan and bake for one hour or until a knife inserted in the center of the loaf comes out clean. Cool on a wire rack for ten minutes before flipping out of pan. I always wrap my loaf in plastic wrap while it is still warm to insure moistness.

Smeared with a layer of cream cheese and enjoyed with a cup of hot Earl Grey tea with honey, persimmon-hickory nut bread cannot be beat as a late fall treat!

PERSIMMON COOKIES

While we're on the subject of persimmons, here's a recipe for cookies that I got from my neighbor Jerry Hanger. They, too, are moist and delicious and easy to make.

½ cup solid vegetable shortening

1½ cups sugar

1 egg

1 teaspoon baking soda

1 cup persimmon pulp

2 cups flour

½ teaspoon each salt, ground cloves, nutmeg

1 teaspoon each cinnamon, vanilla extract

1 cup each raisins, chopped pecans, dates

Preheat oven to 325 degrees. In a large bowl, beat together shortening and sugar until creamy. Add egg and beat well. Add baking soda to the persimmon pulp, then add, alternating with flour, to the shortening mixture. Stir in salt, cloves, nutmeg, cinnamon, vanilla, raisins, pecans, and dates. Mix well and drop by the teaspoonful onto a greased cookie sheet. Bake for about fifteen minutes. While still warm put into a resealable plastic bag.

WILD ASPARAGUS
AND MOREL MUSHROOMS

Two of my favorite wild edibles together in a simple recipe that's sure to please. Asparagus can be found in early spring growing along fencerows. Once a patch is located, you can go back year after year, since asparagus is a perennial. May is the perfect time to start looking for the budding green stalks. Cut them at ground level with a sharp knife. Long before the tender shoots appear, you can locate where they will grow by simply watching out for last year's dead stalks, which look like straw-colored Christmas trees. Morel mushrooms pop up earlier, usually after rainy weather and warm days starting the first of April and running through May. Their lacy, brain-like texture always reminds me of an inverted pinecone, and their taste . . . well, fried up in a pan of butter, they are ambrosia from heaven. Together, the two are irresistible. Here's a ten-minute recipe that is utterly delicious.

1 pound fresh aspara-
gus, cut in long
strips

½ pound fresh
morel mushrooms

1 clove garlic, cut
fine

butter, enough for
sautéing

Combine ingredients and sauté over low heat. Simmer for ten minutes or until the asparagus starts to wilt. Take out, salt and pepper to taste, and serve immediately.

WINTERGREEN TEA

I love a steaming mug of hot tea laced with honey from our own hives, especially in the winter months, when I can sip it in my rocking chair next to the woodstove. I like all kinds of tea, and there are a variety that you can make from wild edibles. Catnip tea is very soothing right before bedtime and helps you sleep. The distinct flavor of sassafras tea has always been a favorite, too. But tea made from leaves of the wintergreen plant has an aroma and taste that is truly superb.

The plant itself is easily identifiable by the low-to-the-ground, broad, leathery leaves that are a bright glossy green all year round. It grows best in the filtered shade often found at the edges of forests. In late July, it bears a small, white blossom similar to lily of the valley, and, in the fall, shiny red berries appear. Since the berries last all winter, they are a very important food source for deer and grouse. Gather the leaves and dry them to make this fragrant tea. To dry, place the leaves in a brown paper bag and leave them for several days. When they are crisp to the touch, they're ready to use.

Into a saucepan, put a goodly handful of leaves and approximately four cups of water. Bring to a boil, then continue to steep over low heat until the water becomes a dark amber color. The distinctive aroma of wintergreen will fill your kitchen while the tea is simmering. When fully steeped, pour into a cup with a generous dollop of honey and enjoy the fruits of your labors.

RAMPS

In June 1990, Maynard Patterson of Sherando took Rebecca Garris and me to Old House Hollow in West Virginia to dig ramps. Up until that time, I had never heard of this wild edible or knew what they were. Also called the wild leek, ramps are considered to be the sweetest and best of the wild onions, with a mild garlic taste that is very pleasant when eaten with salt like a spring onion or added to any type of dish where onions are called for. A word of warning, however: when eaten, ramps leave a very powerful aroma

Maynard Patterson digging ramps

on the breath that seems to last for an interminable amount of time, so be wary when eating them.

The broad leaves of the ramp plant remind me a little of wild orchids and lilies that grow in the woods. The onion-like bulbs are clustered together much like garlic, and digging them requires a trowel or small digging bar to loosen the rocks that the roots grow around. The smaller the bulb, the sweeter and more tender the taste. Ramps grow in dense, rich woodlands from New England to North Carolina but not in every wooded location. They seem to prefer one specific area and grow there year after year.

Maynard said that he started coming to this one particular spot in West Virginia many years ago and has continued right up to the present. He knows where every ramp festival is held from April through May, even though we dug them in early June. Maynard told us that he puts one or two of the flavorful bulbs in with his canned tomato juice each year, and, I must admit, it gave the juice an earthy, unique taste. He also slices a few of them up to fry in with scrambled eggs, and, when I tried it, they were truly delicious!

In Euell Gibbon's book *Stalking the Wild Asparagus*, there is a recipe for a ramp forager's French Onion Soup that is fabulous. Here's the recipe.

1 cup ramps, thinly sliced

2 tablespoons butter

1 can consommé

1 can water

2 tablespoons cooking sherry (optional)

toast rounds (enough for each bowl)

Parmesan cheese, grated (for garnish)

Sauté the ramps in the butter. Add consommé and water. Simmer for twenty minutes over low heat. You can dress it up a bit at this point by adding the cooking sherry; then ladle the soup into individual bowls. Add a round of toast and sprinkle a little grated Parmesan cheese on top. Place the bowls in a hot oven for a few minutes to let the cheese melt.

STINGING NETTLE

I remember my first introduction to this wild potherb. It was truly memorable. As I walked through the woods, my leg brushed up against a tall green plant, and, instantly, it felt like my leg was on fire. I looked down, fully expecting to see a nest of yellow jackets attacking my flesh. I was surprised to see nothing. Rubbing it did no good, and the pain lasted a good ten or fifteen minutes before subsiding. I told a neighbor what happened and was informed that I had gotten into a patch of stinging nettle or nettle weed. So it was with wary, slit-eyed skepticism that I listened to Burley Mays tell me that the weed was one of the most succulent of all greens when cooked properly.

This potherb, like most wild greens, is at its best when gathered in the spring or when the new growth of leaves is picked later in the summer. Armed with welding gloves, scissors, and a large paper bag, I went out to gather my first crop at Hallie Henderson's house, where there was a big patch of nettles growing out by her spring. Like most greens, it takes a lot of leaves to make a "mess," so I filled the entire bag before returning home. I must admit trepidation the first time I cooked it, and taking the first bite was a lesson in faith, wondering if my mouth would be stung like my leg. What a surprise it was to savor the delicious flavor (and lack of sting) of the cooked nettle. Here's how Burley told me to fix them.

Bring some water to a full boil in a stainless steel or enamel pot. Loosely add the nettle leaves along with, say, six chopped wild onions (you can usually find them growing where the nettles are); cover and cook on medium heat for fifteen to twenty minutes. The nettles, once cooked, will turn a bright emerald green. Drain in a colander and put into a bowl with butter, and season with salt and pepper. The greens are a compliment to any meal, and there are usually no leftovers.

JERUSALEM ARTICHOKES

Also known as sun chokes, Jerusalem artichokes were introduced to European settlers in the seventeenth century by Native
American Indians. When they flower, usually in September, they
produce yellow, sunflowerlike blossoms that generally bloom
through October. The plant produces tubers, much like potatoes,
that can be harvested well into winter and on into spring. Nutri-
tionally, the Jerusalem artichoke is low in calories are a good source
of thiamin and vitamin A, ascorbic acid, iron, niacin, protein, and
fiber. Eaten raw, the artichokes have a mild, nutty flavor, but
cooked they taste like a watery potato, only sweeter. Here is some
easy ways to fix them once they have been dug and washed.

Simmer a batch of tubers in boiling water for fifteen to thirty
minutes, then drain off once they are fork-tender. Add some butter and season with salt, pepper, a little lemon juice, and a sprinkle of parsley. Or, if you peel and thinly slice the raw tubers, they
can be added to salads or stir-fried into oriental dishes. The raw
artichokes will add crunchiness, much like water chestnuts. For an
unusual, potatoless salad, steam a pound of tubers for ten to fifteen
minutes then peel, chop, and add with the whites of two hard-
boiled eggs, red and green chopped peppers, and a stalk of chopped
celery. You can then add other ingredients to your liking, such as
chives, olives, chopped pickle, parsley, etc. Finally, mix with a bit
of mayonnaise and enjoy.

STAGHORN SUMAC LEMONADE

The bright red hairy berries of the staghorn sumac can be made
into a delicious cooling summer lemonade that rivals anything you
can buy at the store. The berries are ripe from June through September. Once you locate the sumac, which is a woody shrub growing in fields or at the edge of forests, pinch off one of the red berries
on the conelike cluster and taste the tangy flavor.

To make a pitcher of "lemonade," strip the berries from the cone or just boil several whole cones in a pan of water for about ten minutes, mashing the berries in the hot water. Strain the juice through several layers of cheesecloth to remove the fine hairs, sweeten with sugar to taste, and refrigerate before serving.

THE DANDY DANDELION

We all know this pesky perennial, the scourge of suburbia, with everyone trying their best to eliminate them with sprays and digging tools. Here in the mountains, we've learned to live with them, and we have our ultimate revenge—not by spraying but by eating them!

"Abused, but not used" is one way of describing this most flavorful plant. The entire plant is edible, and, because of its abundance, it is easy to gather a large amount in a short period of time (usually right in your yard). Here are several delicious recipes for you to try the next time you get the urge to rid your lawn of these hearty yellow flower suns.

Dandelion Blossom Fritters

¼ cup of milk

1 teaspoon baking powder

½ cup flour

pinch of salt

1 egg, beaten

2 tablespoons powdered milk

16 large fresh dandelion blossoms (minus stems)

Mix all ingredients together except the blossoms. Wash the blossoms lightly, then drain; dip immediately into batter. Fry until golden brown.

Dandelion Greens

Use the young, tender leaves. Wash
and eat raw with salad dressing; steam
and season with salt, pepper, and butter; or fry up wilted-lettuce style with a
hard-boiled egg.

Dandelion Jelly

4 cups dandelion
blossoms, picked
fresh in the morning

1 quart water

1 package powdered
pectin

2 tablespoons lemon
juice

4½ cups sugar

yellow food coloring

Hold each blossom by its green base
and snip off the golden flowers with
scissors into a saucepan. Discard the
stem. Boil blossoms in water for
three minutes. Drain off three cups
of liquid. Add pectin and lemon
juice to the remaining liquid. When
it comes to a rolling boil, add sugar
and a few drops of yellow food coloring. Boil about three minutes longer
or until it gets to the jelly stage, then
ladle into hot canning jars.

Dandelion Root

Use just like you would parsnips or carrots. Peel, slice, and simmer with a
pinch of baking soda until almost fork-
tender. Drain, then add new water and
simmer until completely tender. Drain
one last time and season with salt,
pepper, and butter, and serve.

ACORNS

Did you know that most acorns are edible? There are approximately fifty varieties of sweet and bitter acorns around the country, and all are easy to gather in the fall months. The only difference between the sweet and bitter nuts is the amount of tannin they contain. But tannin is water-soluble, and the bitterness can be removed by rinsing the acorns in water. Once you come home with your find, rinse them off, and put them into boiling water. Let them boil for ten minutes. This will make them easier to peel. After the shells are removed, scrape as much of the dark membrane off the nuts as you can. Put the shelled acorns in another pot and boil for another ten minutes; any remaining skin should just rub off. Rinse in cold water until the water runs clear. The acorns will have a sweet, cashewlike flavor at this point. Put them into the oven on a flat pan and bake them at 350 degrees for a few minutes to remove moisture. Allow the nuts to cool, then put them in a food processor to create acorn flour or meal. Three cups of acorns yield one cup of meal. Use this meal as you would flour. Here's a great recipe for acorn stuffing:

4 cups bread (torn in pieces)

1¼ cup milk

1 poultry liver, lightly fried and mashed

¼ cup chopped parsley

½ cup diced celery

¼ teaspoon salt

½ teaspoon poultry seasoning

½ cup acorn meal

Thoroughly mix bread and milk together until blended. It should look like cooked cereal. Add the other ingredients and mix well. Stuff the cavity of a chicken or turkey, and roast as you would any other holiday bird.

WILD GRAPE JUICE AND JELLY

We are very fortunate to have an abundance of wild grapes (both fox and coon) growing near our cabin. In the fall, we can sit on the back porch and smell the heady sweet aroma of the fruit that comes wafting down across the Parkway, letting us know the grapes are there for the picking. If you've never eaten wild grape jelly, then let me tell you, the flavor outshines any expensive commercial brand you can find. Hazel Phillips of Nellysford gave me her unbeatable grape juice recipe that even a child can make. I'll give you both versions below.

Annie Coffey making homemade grape juice

For juice as a drink: Take half-gallon or quart canning jars which have been thoroughly washed and put them in a hot water bath until you're ready to use them. Boil the lids and rings and keep them simmering until the juice is ready. Stem all the grapes off the clusters and wash under cold water. To a half-gallon jar (which I always use because it yields more juice) add two cups of whole grapes and one cup of sugar. Cover with boiling water and seal with hot lids and rings. I hold the jar with a towel and turn it upside-down a few times to dissolve the sugar. That's it! Put the jars in the pantry or cellar for a few weeks (longer if you can stand the wait). Refrigerate the jar for a few hours before drinking.

Folks, the result is a crystal clear grape juice that leaves people wondering what your secret ingredient is. Hazel says that she adds half grape juice and half Wink grapefruit soft drink to each glass to stretch out the juice a little, but I like mine straight. To make just a quart of the liquid, cut the recipe in half, using only one cup of whole grapes to half a cup of sugar. The best part is that the whole grapes are infused with the sugar while the juice is "steeping" and can be popped into the mouth as a treat while you drink the liquid! I also use this same recipe to make blackberry juice, since we have a lot of them growing on our place, too.

To make juice for jelly: I make juice for jelly in the fall, then make the jelly itself in early spring when it's not so hot. I wash, stem, and crush the ripe grapes. Use half a cup of water to four quarts prepared grapes. Heat ten minutes at simmering. Do not boil. Drain through a damp jelly bag or several layers of cheesecloth. Then can the juice by bringing it to a simmer and pouring the hot juice into hot jars, leaving a quarter inch of room at the top. Adjust the lids. Process pints and quarts ten minutes in a boiling water bath.

To make jelly: Use three cups of grape juice, one package of powdered pectin, and four cups of sugar. Combine grape juice and pectin in a large saucepan. Bring mixture to a rolling boil. Stir in sugar and return to a rolling boil. Boil hard for one minute, stirring constantly. Remove from heat. Skim foam off if necessary. Pour hot into hot, sterilized jars, leaving a quarter inch of headspace. Adjust lids. Process five minutes in boiling water bath. You'll get about five cups.

These are just a few of the wild edible recipes I've used over the years, but there are many more to chose from. The best and safest way to collect wild edibles of any kind is to get a book that describes each plant in detail and, preferably, has a photo. Better yet, go with a seasoned gatherer who knows the difference between plants that are edible and those that aren't. Gathering wild edibles is one of the most rewarding pastimes a person can have, and the benefits of eating healthy foods from nature is the icing on the cake!

Paulus Fitgerald's barn, Irish Creek, Virginia

Pat Haden of Love, Virginia, hunting for morel mushrooms

13

Morel Mushroom Hunting

One of the first wild foods I learned to identify after moving to the Love community was the morel mushroom. My father used to tell me how he and my grandfather would go out early in the spring to gather the delicate, delectable mushrooms that grew in the woods near their home in Pennsylvania. I was always afraid to guess which mushrooms were and were not poisonous until I learned about the morel. Its unusual shape and texture affords one a pretty good chance of picking a nonpoisonous variety, although there is a "false" morel that you have to look out for (*Gyromitra esculenta*). Once again, the best way to safely harvest mushrooms is to get a good book with photos on the subject or ask to go along with a longtime mushroom hunter who knows what they're looking for.

The distinctive honeycombed texture of its dome-shaped cap leaves no doubt that it is an edible morel. The highly prized, earthy flavor of this particular mushroom makes it one of the most desirable to forage for in the woodlands. Some say morels taste similar to oysters; the older mountain people called it "mountain chicken." Winter snows lying long and heavy can make for a good crop the following spring. From late March to the end of May, depending on the weather, is when "shroomers" hit the woods in search of morels. When the trillium, Dutchman's breeches, violets, and wild strawberries appear, usually so do these mushrooms.

It is estimated that fifty million people around the world actively seek the elusive mushroom.

Morels can be found most anywhere: in fields, near old apple orchards, wooded areas, and by streams. They are highly unpredictable; they may pop up in one location only to completely abandon that spot the next year in favor of another, richer area. But as a general rule, if you find them in one spot, there's a good possibility that they can be found growing there again the next year.

I have a fond memory of a good friend and I who had gone morel hunting in the early 1980s. We had been out combing the woodlands nearly all day without much success only to go back home and find a large patch of them growing along the side of his driveway! Over the years, we always had a good laugh over it and knew exactly where to look for them in successive years.

Morel mushrooms poking up through the ground

Don't expect to find morels easily, especially the first couple of times you try. They seem to blend into their surroundings better than anything else growing in the woods. They take on camouflage that any turkey hunter would be proud to imitate. But like anything else, practice makes perfect; the more you go, the better your eye will be for finding them. The only thing I find hard about hunting morels is the "dizzy" feeling I always get from scanning the forest floor in search of them. They are easier to spot if you slowly glance around the landscape about ten to twenty feet ahead of you instead of trying to look for them straight down. The best things I have found to do is to find a good rock or tree stump and plop yourself down for a few minutes and slowly scan the ground around you. Look for the telltale elongated dome cap that the morel sports. Put everything else out of your mind and try to envision the morel in front of you. Once you find one, more will be in the same vicinity.

And remember, like ginseng hunters, mushroom hunters are very secretive about their "spots." If they divulge where they find morels, sure as anything somebody will beat them to their spot the next season and pick them all. One good thing about morel mushrooms is that they have a sequence in their growing season, so even if you pick them all, you can come back in a few days to find more.

A fine "mess" of morels

The first morels to appear are almost black in color. As the season progresses, they can range in color to brown, gray, yellow, and white; the white ones are some of the largest mushrooms of this variety. Black morels tend to grow in hardwood forests but not around any particular tree. White morels appear later and have a more diverse range of habitat. Forests, fields, old orchards, fencerows, and floodplains are just some of the places these giant morels can be found. The white variety also tend to congregate around certain types of trees; usually bigger, older trees, such as elm, ash, sycamore, and poplar, that are in some stage of dying. As these trees die, the root systems break down, and their nutrients make fertile ground in which morels thrive.

We have always used empty bread bags to gather mushrooms in, but studies have proven that soft mesh bags or a loosely woven basket are the best things to gather them in. This allows their spores to drop back onto the forest floor to replenish the morel population for the next year. Some say that if you gently "tap" the top of the mushroom before putting it into a container, it will ensure that the spores will go back into the soil.

Morels can be frozen successfully if you half-sauté them in a frying pan with butter or olive oil at a fairly high temperature. The liquid from the mushrooms will create a "soup." Remove from heat, put in resealable plastic bags, and freeze. To reuse, put the frozen mixture into a hot frying pan and finish sautéing them.

Butch Allen picking morels

These mushrooms can also be dried. One to two ounces of dried mushrooms equals about a pound of fresh. When needed, simply rehydrate by soaking the morels in wine, milk, soup stock, or water. Use the remaining liquid in recipes.

Butch Allen says that he has been hunting morels for about thirty-five years in Virginia (in Augusta, Nelson, Rockbridge, and Amherst counties) and in Tennessee when he lived there. He says that warm, damp nights and warm daytime temperatures make for a good crop from the first of April to mid-May. He says that the biggest morel he ever found was of the white variety, which he found growing on a mountain in Nelson County about fifteen years ago. When the white morels appear, it signals the close of the mushroom season. Butch pinches the mushroom off the stem at ground level and leaves the root in the soil. He later soaks the morels in salt water for a few hours before draining and rolling them in flour to pan-fry them in butter. But there are all kinds of ways to fix them. Here are a few recipes that I've collected and used through the years.

CREAM OF MOREL SOUP

½ cup butter

⅓ cup chopped onion

¼ cup flour

4 cups hot chicken broth

pinch of nutmeg

1 bay leaf

2 teaspoons butter

½ pound fresh morels, chopped

1 egg yolk

½ cup whipping cream

Melt the half cup of butter in a one-quart, heavy bottomed saucepan; add onions and cook slowly until onions are transparent. Add flour, stir over low heat for three minutes; then add the hot chicken broth, nutmeg, and bay leaf. Whip until all lumps are gone. Bring to a boil; simmer slowly for twenty minutes, then strain.

Heat a large skillet, add two teaspoons butter and morels. Cook over high heat until morels turn gray, but do not brown. Add to soup and simmer ten minutes more. Just before serving, heat soup up to boiling point. In a separate large hot bowl, mix egg yolk with cream. Start adding hot soup, whipping steadily with a wire whisk. When half of soup is added, pour it all back into the remaining soup in the same saucepan and stir. Do *not* bring back to a boil because this will cause it to curdle. Serve immediately.

FRIED MORELS

There are many variations on how to fry these mushrooms. One of the easiest I've found is to just heat up some olive oil or butter, add thinly sliced cloves of garlic, and then fill the pan with morels. Fry quickly at a high temperature, then serve with a steak. Or take a large batch of fresh morels, slice them long ways, and dip in an egg batter. Roll them in seasoned flour, cornmeal, corn flake crumbs, or Ritz or saltine cracker crumbs, then fry in a preheated skillet in real cow butter. Simple, but great!

MOREL MUSHROOM QUICHE

¼ pound bacon

1 pound morels, chopped

½ cup chopped onion

½ cup chopped green pepper

1½ cups shredded Swiss cheese

1½ cups milk

¾ cup biscuit mix

3 eggs

1 teaspoon salt

¼ teaspoon black pepper

Preheat oven to 400 degrees. Cut bacon into small pieces and fry until crisp. Leave in the pan without turning down heat or draining. Add morels. As they cook, it will create a soupy liquid. Cook until the liquid is clear, then drain. In a ten-inch, lightly greased pie pan, mix bacon and mushroom mixture with onion, green pepper, and cheese. In a medium bowl, add milk, biscuit mix, eggs, salt, and pepper. Beat until smooth, then pour mixture over the morel mix. Bake for thirty-five minutes or until an inserted knife comes out clean. Serves 6.

GRILLED MORELS

Season mushrooms with seasoning salt and lay on the grill for just a few minutes. Goes great with burgers or steak. They're easy to fix and so delicious!

Fresh canned pickled beets

14

Pickling Beets

The first time I ever saw people boiling down beets to make beet pickle was when I watched my future mother- and father-in-law, Annie and Saylor Coffey, do it. They were in the side yard, stirring a large cast-iron kettle full of beets on an open fire. After years of making them on the kitchen stove, heating up the whole kitchen, I now realize that boiling them outdoors is the best way to do a large batch. It wasn't until I married their son Billy that Annie gave me her recipe for pickled beets; by far, her way of fixing them is the best I've ever tasted. The recipe is fairly simple after you've finished digging, washing, and cooking the beets. We make a lot of them, since we grow a row or two of the vegetables in our garden each year. You can make a smaller batch if you buy beets at the store or fresh from the various summer farmer markets.

Pickled beets are a welcome addition to any meal, and the homemade kind has a tangy, sweet/tart taste that our family loves. This year, our middle granddaughter Renea wanted to learn how to make them. Because we never turn down free help in the garden, I told her to come on up. As it turned out, I had three free laborers: Renea, her mom Audrey, and her good friend Alex, who did the entire batch of beets with just a few instructions from the sideline. All total, we ended up with thirty-nine quarts of the dark red beauties, and everyone went home with a quart or two. We eat them any old time, but at Thanksgiving and Christmas, all the kids want them on the table for the holiday meal. Here's how we do it.

The first step is to dig your beets out of the garden when they are ready to pull. You can tell when they are ready by peeking under the leaves and checking on the size. The beets are only half buried in the ground, so you can see how big they are before pulling them. Some folks like them medium sized, others prefer to let them grow bigger. It's just personal preference.

Beets in the ground, ready to be pulled

The next step is to cut the tops off, but be sure to just cut the stems down to about half an inch from the beet; *do not* cut into the flesh itself. If you do, the red color will "bleed" out, and you'll have pale looking vegetables. *Do not* cut the skinny, dangly end of the root of the beet either for the same reason. Oh, and before I forget, the leaves (or "greens," as we call them) are delicious to eat, too. Simply pick the small tender ones, put in a pot of water, and

cook as you would any other type of greens. I usually change the water once, since it will have a pinkish cast to it otherwise.

Going back to the beets themselves, the next step is to thoroughly wash them. We do ours outside with the hose in a five-gallon bucket. When clean, bring them in and put them in a large pot and bring to a boil. Once they come to a boil, turn the heat down to medium, cover, and cook until you can poke a long barbecue fork into them easily.

Skinning beets after boiling

The beet-cutting brigade: (L—R) Audrey Coffey, Alex Turner, Renea Coffey

Adding spices

When tender, pour off the water (which will be very dark red) and let cold water run into the pot over the hot beets. Once you are able to handle them, use your hands to slip the skins off and slice or cut into chunks and put them back into a large pot. Pour enough white vinegar into the pot to just cover the beets, add sugar to taste (for a large canning pot, we put in at least five pounds of sugar, sometimes more) and about two large tablespoons of pickling spice, which can be bought in the spice section of the supermarket. Or, for a better bargain that will last many years, go to your local bulk food store, such as the Cheese Shop in Stuarts Draft, and buy a medium-sized bag for a dollar or two.

Bring the mixture to a boil, stirring to dissolve sugar, then ladle into hot canning jars (we use quarts), and adjust the lids and rings, which have been soaking in the hot water with the jars. Put the

Ladling hot beets into canning jars

hot jars somewhere out of a draft, and let them seal. When you hear the familiar "ping" of the lids sealing, you'll know they're ready for the pantry shelves.

Like anything else, the longer you leave the beets before eating, the better the taste, since they will have had more time to be infused with the juice. That's all there is to it. If you decide to give it a try, you'll be rewarded with the best-tasting pickled beets you've ever eaten. If Renea can do it, you can too!

15

Plain Folk & Simple Livin'

Throughout *Backroads* newspaper's twenty-five-year existence, I wrote a column entitled "Plain Folk & Simple Livin'," which highlighted many of my experiences living here in Love, Virginia. The readers seemed to love the everyday adventures of a rural mountain housewife, many of which were so awful they were humorous. I am including one article that people have asked to be reprinted again and again. Enjoy the laugh and remember,

"DO NOT ATTEMPT THIS AT HOME!"

THE GREAT WALNUT-HULL DYE JOB

A few weeks ago, I ran into a former coworker; after we exchanged a few pleasantries, she took it upon herself to delicately inform me of my hair's advancing grayness. Actually, what she said was, "Boy! You've *really* gotten gray since I last saw you!" I thought to myself, thank you so very much for bringing that bit of unwelcome news to my attention.

She was right up there with my mother, who, when I'd bend over to tie her shoes, would tap my head with her index finger and announce, "Where'd all that gray come from?"

I tell people, now that I am over the advanced age of fifty, that it is only natural for a few strands of silver to be mixed in with the brown color of my hair.

There was a time when my daughter Heather would make me sit on the floor in front of her while she searched for the offending white hairs and pluck them out. Now she says that if she were to continue doing that, I'd soon be bald. Once again, many thanks.

The hairdressers weren't much better. Each time I'd go to get my hair cut, they'd start badgering me about putting in a little color. When they'd hit a wall of resistance on my part, the compromise would begin. "Maybe we could put a rinse on it . . . to temporarily hide the gray. The color would wash out after a few shampoos." I didn't see the sense in "temporarily" hiding an obvious fact, and there was the argument that I'd have to keep coloring once I started. I've also noticed that these women are positively possessed when it comes to color, because each time I come in, their hair is a different hue. It seems to excite them. It scares me. In fact, I actually changed beauty salons right after the girl who always heckles me about coloring my hair dyed her own once too often, and it broke off like raw spaghetti.

I remember the day I got a call from our youngest daughter Rebecca, who is a beautician, saying she had "gone blond" in a big way. What she actually said, between sobs, was, "I look like a banana!"

Maybe it's age. Maybe it's indifference. Maybe it's just because I am now over fifty and am not swayed by everyone else's opinion of what is socially correct, but I have no desire to cover my graying hair. At least, not from a bottle.

I am what you'd call a natural girl. Never one to slather on makeup, get my nails done, or wear my tresses in fancy styles. But there was a time that I decided to do something to stop those advancing wiry white hairs by using a natural product.

Each fall, we had an accumulation of black walnuts that fell from our trees. I noticed that when we ran over the nuts with the wheels of our truck, a thick, dark-brown substance oozed out onto the ground. Closer inspection revealed that the goo didn't have a bad odor, and it had the consistency of kindergarten paste.

So one night I told my daughter that I was going to mix up a concoction of the thick brown slime to dye my hair.

There was no manual for this homemade project. No directions to follow. It was just one of those (if you'll excuse the pun) "hair brained" ideas that I am known to come up with from time to time.

So, while my daughter was in school, I went out and gathered a goodly number of walnut hulls and began a cooking process in the kitchen, boiling the husks down to a thick sauce. When Heather came home, I showed her my handiwork and asked her to come into the bathroom to supervise the dyeing process. She watched with interest as I began pouring the walnut puree over my hair, working it in extra good with my bare hands to make sure each strand of hair was well saturated. I hunkered over the tub a good ten or fifteen minutes, letting the brown tea steep into my roots. I began to get excited about this new natural hair dye. I mean, what brunette wouldn't want a way to cover her gray without harsh chemicals and expensive salon prices? Dollar signs started flashing in my eyes. Purely by mistake and through home-made experimentation, I just may have hit on something to give Miss Clairol a run for her money!

When it came time to rinse, I put my head under the faucet until my hair ran clean. Then I wrapped a towel around it and stood up triumphantly, turning toward Heather. For a moment, she just stood there looking blank. Then her face took on a funny look, and I noticed that her mouth was frozen into a silent "O." I knew something was terribly amiss. Looking in the mirror, I saw with horror what Heather was staring at. My hair was beautiful, dyed a luxurious brown, which I couldn't have been more pleased with. But that same shade of dark walnut was now embedded into the skin of my forehead, neck, and hands! My fingernails looked like I had been digging in the coalfields. Repeatedly. For long periods of time.

Try as I might, no amount of scrubbing seemed to remove the stain. I even tried dabbing pure bleach on it to no avail. My natural permanent hair color was just that—permanent. So, for the next six weeks, although I got some nice compliments on my hair, I'm sure everyone talked behind my back about my lack of personal hygiene. The only thing that saved me from total embarrassment was that the episode happened during late autumn, so I could wear turtlenecks and gloves to hide my shame.

There you have it. Lynn's homemade attempt at hair color. Unless they come up with something a little easier and a tad bit gentler, I am going to go gray naturally, no matter how many times my mother taps my head!

Cabin in Love, Virginia

Ethel Inez Small Hughes at her Nellysford home

16

Ethel Inez Small Hughes

Nellysford, Virginia

T his article originally appeared in the February 2000 edition
of *Backroads* newspaper. Inez Hughes has since passed away.
I hope you enjoy her story as much as I enjoyed interviewing her.

Except for the brief time she stayed at her sister's house in Richmond and during her honeymoon, Inez Hughes has the distinc-
tion of being born, raised, and living her whole life in the very
same place. That's a big accomplishment for someone who will be
celebrating her ninety-sixth birthday on February 3, 2000.

Born the seventh child in a family of fourteen, Edith Inez
Small made her way into the world on a cold February day in
1904. She was the third daughter of Adolphus "Dahl" Glenroy
Small and his wife Nancy "Nanny" Henderson Small. The pater-
nal side of the family came from Ireland, while her mother's great-
grandfather came from Germany and her great-grandmother
hailed from England.

Inez's parents were married in 1889 at a church along Back
Creek in Augusta County, where her mother's family lived. Her
father's family lived in the Adial area of Nelson County. After
their marriage, Adolphus and Nancy lived with relatives for a few
years before settling on Route 664 on the east side of the Blue

Ridge Mountains, down below where the Clarence Campbell family lived in Nelson County. The family lived there for five years before moving to a home in Nellysford in 1904. The home-place was located just behind where the present Stoney Creek Medical Center now stands. Inez was the first child to be born in the new home.

Her siblings included four sisters, Lola, Nettie, Bessie, and Christine, and nine brothers, Carl, Pearson, Bosba, Harmon, Leverett, Stanley, Lowell, Alvin, and Algernon. Bessie died when she was eighteen months old from a disease known as the "bloody flux." Algernon succumbed to croup at age four, and Lowell died at seven years of age from complications of the dreaded childhood disease, infantile paralysis, or polio. Of the original fourteen, only two still survive: Inez and her sister Christine, who is now ninety years of age.

Originally, Ethel's name was Edith, but as she grew older, she thought that the name sounded too much like the word "idiot," so she changed it to Ethel but continued to be called by her middle name. Her mother, however, always called her "Ida," and, today, her grandchildren all call her by the nickname "Nez," since Inez felt that she was too young to be called "grandma" when they came along.

Growing up, Inez recalls that their household was "plumb full and running over" with children. "Mama never knew how many she'd be cooking Sunday breakfast for because the boys were always inviting their friends over to spend Saturday nights." Breakfast consisted of fried ham and bacon, eggs, oatmeal, hoecakes, and huge stacks of pancakes "as big

Courtesy of Inez Hughes

Some of the Small family: (L–R, back row) Bosba, Pearson, Carl, Fleetie (Carl's wife), Thelma (their baby); (center) Leverett, Harmon; (front) Nanny, Stanley, Adolphus, Lowell

around as a bowl." Inez said that they disappeared as fast as her mother could make them.

"My mother was a wonderful cook, and in making cakes, people would ask how she'd know how much flour and such to put in, to which she'd reply, 'I put in till I think it's enough!'"

With all those children to dress, I asked if her mother sewed their clothes. I was surprised to learn that the family bought ready-made garments in Waynesboro. At first, her parents would make the trip in a horse and buggy, staying overnight with people in town before returning the next day. But in 1917, the Adolphus Small family bought their first car, and the trip to Waynesboro was made in one day. While still on the subject of clothing, Inez told a humorous story about her mother as a young woman, trying her best to get the hang of handling the hoop that was sewn into the hem of dresses in the 1800s. She said that her mother was about fifteen years old, already courting her future husband, when she sat down at church and forgot to adjust the hoop. As she sat on the pew, the hoop came up, causing her dress to fly over her head. "She was so embarrassed because my father was there in church and saw the whole episode."

When Inez was growing up, her father, Adolphus Small, was a farmer by trade, raising cattle and tobacco. He then became a lumberman, cutting timber in the mountains surrounding his home and hauling it on trucks to a sawmill in Crozet. He owned several sawmills in the area, and later on, when his sons were grown, they helped to operate them. In the early years, he also cut tanbark and hauled it to Lyndhurst with a team of oxen. One night, when a storm came up, Adolphus unhooked the oxen and took shelter inside a church along the way. With the lightning flashing, he thought he saw something coming up the center isle of the church, which scared him so badly that he fled. Later, he realized that it was probably just another man seeking shelter inside the church during the storm.

Inez attended Rockfish Valley Elementary School, which covered grades 1–7, and later the Rockfish Valley High School to finish grades 8–10. Children didn't start school back then until they were seven years old. She remembers her first teacher as being a Miss Susie Higginbotham, who was a kindly woman who later married Forest Hughes and lived in the large white house on Route 151, across from the present bank in Nellysford. Other teachers included Gertha Bishop, Myrtle Bailey, and Annie Page, who taught the high school grades. Inez laughs at the thought of how easily embarrassed Annie Page always was and a certain incident that almost put her over the edge emotionally.

One day, as the class was having morning devotions, Annie was standing up front and the button popped off her under drawers. They fell to the floor in full view of the class. She was so embarrassed that she cried and had to go home. The next day, some of the big boys had put a huge safety pin on her desk, and it upset her so badly that she left and didn't return for two more days.

The boys also used to dip the girls' braids in the inkwells. Inez remembers two boys who had been out hunting the night before and killed a polecat. To cover the smell before they came to school, they stopped off at the store and bought a bottle of cheap, ten-cent cologne and splashed it all over themselves. The teacher sent both of them home because she said she could stand the stink of polecat better than she could the two mixed together.

School subjects back then were English, algebra, geometry, physical geography, calculus, history, English literature, and spelling. For spelling, they'd have to spell the word one day and give the definition the next. Inez felt that children got a good education in her day. "We had to know it! Nowadays they got computers to do everything." Along those lines, Inez told another humorous story about her brothers walking down the long lane to the store until their father bought his car. "Then they wouldn't walk anymore . . . they wanted to drive. Daddy said, 'Confound it, after a while babies will soon be born without legs because they won't know how to walk.' I say today's children will soon be born without brains because computers are doing all their thinking!"

As children, Inez said that they had a lot of fun. They played everything from baseball and jackrocks to checkers and Rook. They swam in the deep hole of the Rockfish River and got together on Saturday evenings to make candy or popcorn while someone played the organ, and they all sang. I about fell off my chair when Inez asked if I had ever played "post office." She kidded and asked, "You know, that game where the boys get to kiss the girls?" I smiled and replied, "Yes, Inez, I remember it."

The family attended Wintergreen Christian Church or Adial Baptist Church, and Inez recalled that they held Sunday school and worship services but had no mid-week service back then. They did, however, have one-week and two-week revivals during the summer months. She remembers some of the early preachers at Wintergreen Christian Church as being Mr. Watson, Reilly Fitzgerald, and Pettit Coffey. Some arrived on horseback, and they stayed with her parents during the revival week. On Sunday, they'd have a service and afterward have a huge dinner-on-the-grounds luncheon. She remembers that the first time she ever saw a cake with different-colored layers was at one of these revival luncheons. "It was baked by a Mrs. Reynolds, and it had pink and chocolate layers, but you couldn't see them until the cake was cut because of the icing."

Because Adial Baptist Church was farther away, the congregation built a sister church, Rockfish Valley Baptist Church, closer to Nellysford, so that the people from the community could worship without having to travel such a great distance.

As a young girl, Inez had long, dark brown, naturally curly hair. "All my brothers and sisters had curly or wavy hair except one sister. She wore her hair in plaits that she wrapped around her head, which was the style back then. Later she cut it short when 'bobs' were all the rage."

Inez's parents strictly forbade her to formally date until she was

From right to left: Inez, her niece Eileen, and her sister Christine

sixteen years old. She said, "I thought I'd *never* get to be sixteen! Of course I used to court a bit on the sly, like all kids do." She remembers her first boyfriend as being Lacy Bradley.

My brother was courting his sister, so I'd go along when he'd go to visit, just to see Lacy, you know? Or I'd see some boys at school or church. If a boy would come to the house to visit and stayed later than ten o'clock at night, Daddy would embarrass me by coming in the room and sitting down and winding his watch. If they didn't take the hint and leave, he'd say, "It's time for all honest folks to be in bed."

Although I had known Carleton Hughes my whole life, he was six years older than I, so he never took notice of me until I was around fifteen years old. He had gone to service for three years, and, in that time, I kind of grew up. When he came home, we were both at a community carnival, and he asked who that "pretty girl" was. We would visit back and forth some, but we couldn't really start courting until I was sixteen. I graduated from Rockfish Valley High School, and I remember I wore a pink dress to the commencement exercises that were held at the Presbyterian Church. A good friend made my white graduation dress.

Inez had sisters living in Richmond, and, after graduation, she decided to go down and stay with one when she got a job at Miller & Rhodes Department Store. In 1924, Inez and Carleton Hughes were married at a preacher's home in Richmond, and they left on a honeymoon to Newport News, where Carleton sought employment at the shipyards. When he learned that they weren't hiring, they went on to West Virginia, where he signed on to work in the coalmines. But one look inside the dark, damp mines was enough to convince him that he didn't want to work underground. He came back and told his wife, "Pack your clothes, we're going home."

The couple set up housekeeping in a little house on Spruce Creek that belonged to Carleton's family. They lived there for five years before building a home in Nellysford, moving there in 1929

with their only child, Margaret
Joyce. Joyce said that though she was
just a little child, she can remember
her mother and herself walking from
Spruce Creek every day to where her
father was building the new house to
watch the progress. A man by the
name of Walter Snead, who was a
tinner, put the metal roof on the new
home.

*Inez at her high-school graduation with
future husband, Carleton Hughes*

At first, Inez said, her husband
had an orchard, but the drought of
1930–31 dashed their hopes of making a living from their fruit
trees. Carleton became a carpenter, since he had a natural talent
for that craft. He worked in the building trade, as well as being a
farmer, until he retired. The family raised all their own food, so
the Great Depression didn't affect them as much as it did the people living in the cities. "We had pork, beef, and chickens, as well
as a large variety of fruits and vegetables which we put up. The
government gave us ration coupons for gas, coffee, sugar, and flour,
according to how many were in the family. The country people
with large families fared better than most."

Joyce, being the only child, remembers her parents with fondness and says that she never heard them argue. Inez, in turn, said,
"I once visited a family who always fussed, and I said if I got married, I wasn't ever going to fuss like that. And I never did."

The Rockfish River was at the rear of their property, but Inez
said that she could only remember it flooding the basement once.
The family got electric service in 1939, and Inez remembers that
the road in front of their house was hard surfaced in 1940.

The Hugheses were a close-knit and happy family who lived
life to the fullest. When Joyce married Herbert Ward, her parents
gave them land adjoining theirs, and the couple built a home just
up the road. That meant that Carleton and Inez were close enough
to enjoy the five grandchildren who were born to Joyce and Herbert. Although Carleton passed away in 1977, Inez continued to

live an active, independent life in the years that followed. The far-thest away a family member lives is in Troy, Virginia.

I asked Inez about the changes she's seen in her ninety-six years, and they were numerous. Number one in her book is the way parents now raise their children. "It used to be that the parents would tell the children what to do. Now the kids seem to be telling the parents. If we'd have talked to my mother and daddy like they do today, we'd have been eating teeth for the next few days!"

Crime is something else that Inez feels is more prevalent. "The worst crime back then was if a man got a young woman pregnant. The law would catch the man responsible and make him marry her or else he'd go to jail. He had to support her, you know?"

On fashion, Inez said that she wore a bathing suit that covered more of her body than today's styles. "Now all they have is a string! And I know a man who says he's been watching the hemlines ris-ing and the necklines falling for years, and he's living for the day they meet in the middle."

After we got done laughing, Inez said that she has always loved living in the country. She felt like country folks thought more of each other and did more for each other than their city counter-parts. She feels that God is still in control and should be an inte-gral part of people's lives. "There is always something to be thankful for." Inez is thankful for her daughter Joyce, her five grandchildren, twelve great-grandchildren, and her one great-great-grandchild.

God has blessed Inez Hughes with good health, a tremendous humor, an incredible memory, a kind and loving heart, and a posi-tive attitude, which accounts for her long life and the twinkle in her eye. A special thank you to Inez for sharing her memories and her life with *Backroads* readers. I can truly say that we're all the better for it. May God richly bless you on your ninety-sixth birthday and in the years that follow.

Rock chimney at Coffey homeplace, Chicken Holler

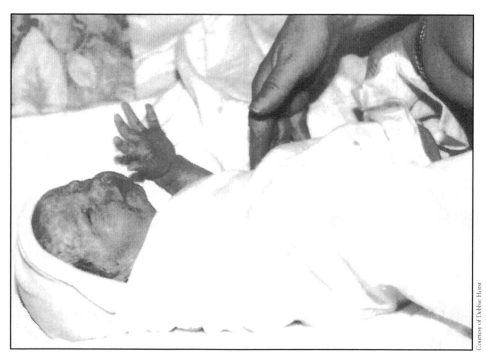

Newborn Jordan Elizabeth Horst

17

Midwives and
Home Births

The May 1998 issue of *Backroads* newspaper was dedicated solely to the ancient profession of midwifery and the women who chose to employ their services. Birthing babies at home is certainly not a new trend. As early as the book of Exodus, it was recorded that midwives helped women in their labor. This was the general rule right up to the early 1900s, when the medical profession gradually began telling the family practice doctors and midwives that they could no longer deliver babies in the home. They explained that they now had specialized medicine and trained doctors in the specifics of childbirth, so all further births would be done in the hospital where they had modern equipment needed for laboring women. Without women even being aware of the subtle change, their roll as an active participant ebbed away, until they are now content, at the onset of labor, to go to the hospital and let doctors deliver their babies.

At first glance, delivery by midwife almost seems a radical act in this day of medical technology. It has somehow been conveyed that childbirth is something like a sickness that must be endured and finally taken care of with the aid of drugs, monitors, and surgical procedures. It's what women have been taught and told to do by their mothers. But if they had gone one generation back and talked to their grandmothers, they would have gotten a far different story.

We are now seeing a resurgence in midwifery and home births as women want more of a say in what should be a natural and gratifying experience. After interviewing the midwives and the girls who chose them over the hospital and after reading more on the subject, I began to see a pattern emerge as to the healthiness of home birth for both the mother and her newborn child.

Statistics show that in some hospitals, there is a 90 percent rate of using epidural drugs as opposed to a 0 percent drug use in home births. Eighty percent of all women who have a hospital delivery also have episiotomies, a cutting of delicate tissues now considered a routine procedure. Midwives record a very low (under 10 percent) episiotomy rate. And a whopping 24 percent of all laboring women end up having a cesarean section at a hospital compared to a modest 4 percent for midwife-assisted births. The women who do need surgery are transported to a hospital where the operation can take place. Midwives are required to have a medical backup in case of emergencies, and they say there is plenty of time to get their client to a medical facility if needed.

What these figures are saying is that, although we have amassed tremendous medical technology and skill during this century, too often procedures are used that aren't necessary, just convenient. It is a known fact that nothing can improve on nature, and God Himself designed the miracle of birth to more or less take care of itself. There is nothing wrong with modern medicine, if used when necessary and not as a substitute for what nature will do for itself in the due process of time.

Many women are not aware of available alternatives, such as home birth or birthing centers. They have simply become a vessel wherein a baby resides until the doctor decides it's time to bring the child into the world. Mothers have lost the joy and triumph of pushing a baby out all by themselves with no artificial help. The intimate miracle of birthing one's own child in the presence of the supportive husband who helped create the new life within will never be improved upon, no matter how much technology we amass.

But now, many mothers-to-be are voluntarily making the same

birth choices their grandmothers did, having their children naturally, knowing how much healthier it is for them and their newborns. They are giving nature a chance to bring to life the drama of childbirth as they reclaim their right to the birth experience.

Come with me now as I talk to three practicing certified nurse midwives, the two young women whose children were delivered by them, and a woman who had her babies at home fifty years ago, delivered by a midwife.

MIDWIFE MARTHA ROHRER
Dayton, Virginia

At a young and vibrant sixty-six years of age, it's not easy for Martha Rohrer to think about retirement. But she says that when she has delivered her one thousandth child or when she turns sixty-seven, whichever comes first, she is going to leave the delivering of babies to the next generation of midwives.

Much respected and widely known, Martha has had a rich and rewarding career as a registered nurse and a certified nurse midwife. She will be sorely missed in medical circles over a widespread area of Virginia.

It all began when, as a young girl, Martha decided on a career in medicine. She went to nursing school, and, at twenty-five years old, she was recruited by the Mennonite Church to accompany three other young women on a trip to Ethiopia where they would practice their profession as missionary nurses. She stayed for sixteen and a half years before finally coming home to take care of her parents in 1975. Upon

Martha Rohrer

returning to Pennsylvania, she found that the daughters of her girl-friends were asking if she would deliver their babies, since they knew that she'd had that type of experience in Ethiopia. Her nursing license would not permit her to deliver babies in the U.S., so she toyed with the idea of going to midwifery school in the future. In 1979, she was accepted at the Meharry Medical College in Nashville, Tennessee, where she received her midwifery training.

Coming back to Pennsylvania, Martha practiced her profession there for ten years before moving to Virginia. She said that at the time she made the move, she was up to the seventh child in the same family for some of her clients. Practicing the last eight years in Virginia (as of 1998), she is now up to five in the same family here.

Martha does only home births in her practice, coming directly to the client's house, making appointments convenient for the mother-to-be. She carries with her a black doctor's bag that was given to her by her family physician, Dr. William Diedrich, who delivered some forty thousand babies in his long career. When he found out that Martha was studying to be a midwife, he gave her the bag, saying, "You might as well have my doctor's bag that's been put away in the attic." Fitted in the bottom of the bag is an antique copper kettle, which can be removed. Instruments can be placed in it and boiled in preparation for the birth. There is also extra gauze and alcohol, which she carries for additional sterilization.

When asked what she likes best about being a midwife, Martha says that it's getting to know each family and building a good rapport with them. She states, "Because it is so personal, there is just something about that type of friendship that goes beyond the doctor/patient relationship. And there's something wonderful about seeing the husbands supporting their wives during labor and delivery . . . being included in the birth. The joy of seeing the parents when the little one is born and watching the siblings come in to hold their new brother or sister is what togetherness as a family is all about."

She says of midwife births that women are happy to be at home in their own bed with familiar surroundings. Martha encourages the girls to find comfortable positions to labor in so that they will be more at ease, thus speeding up the birth process.

"I truly believe that when you have to start thinking about having to get up and get dressed in the middle of the night, finding someplace to put the other children, getting in the car and driving to the hospital, not knowing who is going to take care of you or what is going to happen to you once you arrive, takes its toll on the mother and shuts down labor. Then you have to wait until everything begins again. Then they lay you flat on your back so you can't move. No, I'm sorry, but that is just not the surroundings needed for an easy birth."

Martha is a firm believer of nature, knowing what's best to bring about birth, and she feels that many problems can be attributed to medical interference at the hospital. She says that the more interference with the labor process, the more the body shuts down and makes things harder for the mother all the way around.

If a woman suspects she may be pregnant and wants the services of Martha as a midwife, this is basically what happens. The mother is referred to her family physician to get needed blood work done. At about the fourth or fifth month, Martha makes her first house visit and then schedules monthly visits until the ninth month; then she will switch over to weekly calls until the birth.

Martha gives out childbirth literature and carefully goes over it with the expectant mother, answering any questions that she may have concerning her pregnancy. Martha explains the different stages of labor and what to expect when the baby is due. She tells the woman about the importance of a good prenatal vitamin supplements, exercise, and diet during the months ahead. She says that it is very important to go over these things so that the mother-to-be will be aware of the discomforts and changes she will feel during pregnancy. As the due date approaches, Martha has the woman send off for a birthing kit, which contains a disposable bed covering, four-by-four-inch gauze pads, gloves, a bulb syringe, and a cord clamp.

In her practice, Martha designates Mondays, Wednesdays, and Fridays as visiting days. On Mondays, she covers the Staunton/

Stuarts Draft/Waynesboro areas; Wednesdays she stays in the Dayton area; and Fridays are restricted to the Harrisonburg/North clients. This schedule keeps her busy. She recalls 1988 as a record year where births were concerned. She delivered ninety-eight children that year, putting nearly twenty thousand miles on her car.

She says that there are really no restrictions for a healthy mother. But if a woman has previously had a miscarriage, she will tell her to take it extra easy in the early months, particularly when her period would be due.

Of her most difficult birth, Martha relates how an extra large baby (11.2 pounds) had a hard time coming through the birth canal. Although his head made it out, the child's shoulders became wedged under the pubic bone and tailbone and refused to budge. She got the father and mother to push while she pulled, and eventually the baby made a safe entry.

Martha said of the 882 babies she has delivered thus far, about two-thirds of that number were to girls of the Amish/Mennonite faith. She says that these women, by far, have the easiest labors and births because she thinks they are used to more physical work, such as squatting in the garden and hanging up clothes, which stretch the appropriate muscles and make their deliveries easier.

As with all midwives, when it's time for one of her clients to have a baby, Martha packs a bag and goes to stay with the family until the child arrives. Only after the necessary things are done and the mother and child have had a healing herbal bath, will Martha leave. She has an assistant, Kaye McDonagh, an Irish woman with a British midwife degree, who goes on labor calls with her.

After a birth is over, Martha goes home but returns the very next day to check on how things are going. On the fourth day, she goes back to put the baby's tiny footprints on a birth certificate and to do a blood test that screens for PKU (a genetic disorder that can cause brain damage). She also does little extras, like putting a birth announcement in the newspaper, then clipping it out and sending it to the new parents.

Even after retirement, Martha says she'll continue to go on a few labor calls to some special folks she knows, purely as an observer of another midwife doing the delivery. But she is looking forward to having more time with her husband, Ivan, and having the freedom to take off and do things together. They were married late in life, and, although they have no children of their own, Martha laughs and says that she's pushed and grunted with the best of them and feels like she's had quite a few! She also takes care of her mother, Mary Hartzler, ninety-three, in her home. Like Martha, Mrs. Hartzler certainly doesn't seem to age, keeping busy with several projects at once.

As the interview wound down, I asked Martha who would continue the midwife profession when the older ones started retiring from practice. With a gleam in her eye, she smiled and said with confidence, "God will provide."

MIDWIVES JACKI ROOKE
AND LESLIE STEEVES
Charlottesville, Virginia

Both Jacki Rooke, who started the Birth Center of the Blue Ridge in Charlottesville, Virginia, and her partner, Leslie Steeves, were practicing RNs who decided to become midwives as a direct result of their own unsatisfactory birth experiences.

The Birth Center, which opened two years ago [in 1996], is fast becoming an alternative for women wanting to have their babies in a more natural, relaxed way. Its success is apparent by the growing number of births the midwives are seeing at the center. Jacki states that when she first started, she was doing three to four births a month. It's closer to six or seven now, many of which are from repeat mothers coming in for successive children.

Jacki's story begins after she had already gone to nursing school and graduated as a registered nurse. She worked in three different hospitals as an OB nurse and also in the newborn ICU ward before realizing that she didn't like the way the births were handled and felt that birthing didn't belong in a structured environment such as a hospital. In 1983, she began thinking about going back to

Jacki Rooke and Leslie Steeves

school for another year and becoming a certified nurse midwife. This proved harder than she thought, since the school was located in Tennessee, and there were only five openings for more than four hundred applicants. It took three years to get in, and, once accepted, her family had to move to Tennessee so that she could finish her schooling. People started calling before she even had her midwifery degree, wanting information on home births and trying to schedule appointments.

The Rooke family moved back to Charlottesville, and Jacki began her midwife career, working out of her own home and doing home births. In the years she has been delivering babies, she has discovered many things, such as how out of touch women are with their own bodies and their own needs.

Jacki states, "Women have not asked their mothers and their grandmothers any questions about their experiences on having children, so we have become ignorant and misinformed about the whole birth process. It's hard to keep things natural because of the way we have been taught, along with our own natural fears. Also, I am becoming more aware of how physiological problems, such as abuse that hasn't been dealt with, will trigger a slowing process in labor. The obstetric staff in hospitals is quick to go to technology, and it's hard for midwives to practice and promote natural birth under these conditions. I think there is a rising trend to slowly push midwives out of practice."

In the fourteen years that Jacki has been a midwife, she has seen many things. I asked about her most difficult birth, and she said that it involved a woman who was having a lot of bleeding. The decision was made to transport her to a hospital where Jacki has medical backup, and everything turned out fine.

Her longest birth took fifty-two hours, and Jacki stayed with the laboring mother the whole time. In another instance, the baby came before she could get there, and the husband delivered the infant.

Leslie Steeves joined the Birth Center a year ago and went into midwifery for much the same reasons as Jacki—to heal her own unsatisfactory birth experiences. Leslie, an RN, chose to go to the Frontier School in Hyden, Kentucky, to get her midwife degree. But unlike Jacki, she had the option of modular schooling, which meant much of her studies could be accomplished by computer, and the family did not have to make a move. At the end, Leslie did travel to the school to finish her "hands on" requirement of midwife experience before accepting her degree.

She is very happy with the way things are progressing at the Birth Center and says, "Women who have had bad experiences will always push to have future births in a more natural way. I love the personal involvement a midwife has with the whole family. Working as a nurse on a standard eight-hour shift, you don't have that luxury. When you go to a person's home, you get to see them in their own space, and it is a much more relaxed atmosphere."

The Birth Center itself is a very comfortable place that puts one instantly at ease in its homelike surroundings. Photos of newborn babies and their families dot the walls, and there is a feeling of warmth and peacefulness the minute you walk through the door.

The Birth Center was opened to provide an out-of-hospital childbearing area for women who do not desire to give birth at home, yet are not satisfied with the available hospital birthing options. Its goal is to provide safe, satisfying maternity care in a comfortable home atmosphere. Birth is shared with whomever the mother wishes. And in the days and weeks after birth, mothers and babies are followed closely with home visits and telephone calls.

A certified nurse midwife (CNM) is a registered nurse with advanced education in midwifery. They must take a national certifying exam that is administered by the American College of Nurse Midwives, and they are licensed to practice in all fifty states. Currently, there are nearly seven thousand CNMs in the United States. CNMs believe that pregnancy and birth is a normal, healthy process for most women. They are particularly skilled at supporting women through normal pregnancy and birth. Taking the time to develop a personal relationship with a woman and to include the woman in her care is key. Extensive prenatal education is shown to improve maternal/infant outcomes and is highly stressed at the center by both midwives.

When asked who can deliver at the birth center, Jacki is quick to say that it is designed for low-risk, healthy women. Certain medical and obstetrical conditions would not be favorable, such as diabetes, chronic high blood pressure, toxemia, pre-eclampsia, preterm deliveries (before thirty-seven weeks), significantly post-term (beyond forty-two weeks), breech, twins, or any other serious medical condition that could put mother and child at risk.

With the rising cost of having a baby, both home delivery and birth center options make a lot of sense for those who qualify. The trend is taking hold for women wanting to have more say in the birth of their children.

HOME BIRTHS
Katie and F. P. Phillips; Nellysford, Virginia

The Phillipses live in a log cabin situated on a little flat, with a 360-degree view of the Blue Ridge Mountains just outside their door. There is a twenty-year difference in their ages, yet the personalities of Frederick Pershing (F .P., for short) Phillips and his engaging wife Katie have meshed together so tightly, you cannot

think of one without the other. They are a happy couple, under-
taking many large projects that will keep them busy for years to
come. At the time of this writing [1998], they operate Valleymont
Market in Nellysford, and F. P. is perusing a career in nursing. They
are building a large addition onto their cabin to provide space for
their growing family, which includes Zachariah, nearly two years of
age, and little Sarah, eight months.

Perhaps the most amazing thing about them is the fact that
Katie and her husband chose to have both of their children at
home, in the same rural setting that has been home to the Phillips
family for generations. Katie was the inspiration for the midwife
edition of *Backroads* when I learned that both of her children were
born at home.

F. P. and Katie Phillips with their children, Zach and Sarah

Katie was already four months pregnant with Zach when she called Jacki Rooke, a certified nurse midwife, and made her first appointment. Jacki was surprised by Katie's call, since as a rule, she doesn't take first-time mothers. But Katie persisted, and plans were made for her prenatal care and education about home birthing. In Katie's own words, here are the reasons for her decision.

My mother had very short, easy labor with her children, so I didn't have to listen to any nightmare stories about birth. There was nothing to influence me about not being able to do it, and I wanted to have something good to say about the whole experience. Plus, I guess I've always wanted to do something different.

I had several friends who had home births, and they were very positive about it, so I decided to go that route, too. When I found out I was pregnant, I began reading all types of literature about childbirth, and I noticed there was very little about alternatives such as midwife-assisted births and birthing centers. One book did give information about "doulas," women in Ireland whose sole job was to support a woman in labor with massage and comforting words. The article said with a doula, labor was decreased by two or three hours. At the library, I found a book about "husband-coached" childbirth by a Dr. Bradley. His method seemed to be the healthiest way to have a baby. There are all kinds of classes and printed material about natural birthing, so don't wait to be told . . . read up and inform yourself!

I thought to myself, *I trust God, and I trust my body.* After thousands of years that people have been having home births, I decided if I had good prenatal care, there should be absolutely no reason for me not to be able to be successful. Another reason I chose to deliver at home was I felt a lot of times procedures are done unnecessarily in hospitals, and I wanted the healthiest start for our children. Plus I wanted the convenience of being in my own home.

F. P. was behind his wife's decision 100 percent. Being raised on a farm, he felt like birth was a natural process, which more or less took care of itself when the time came. Being in the medical field, he also knew that having a baby at home would be less traumatic on all of them.

Katie and F. P. chose to contact Jacki Rooke when three different people recommended her as a midwife. They both agreed that from the first moment they talked on the phone, they felt totally comfortable with her.

Katie went to the birth center for her monthly checkups until the eighth month; after that she went every two weeks, then every week until her due date. She laughs at the memory of sliding in a few extra visits on one of her pregnancies because she went eighteen days past her due date.

In talking with Katie about her first home birth with their son, Zachariah Christian, born on May 17, 1996, she said that a friend who had had a baby previously, came to assist the midwife during Katie's labor.

> Because of my inexperience, both women helped me to know when to push and when not to push. It was the first time my body was meeting that kind of challenge, so I was glad for their knowledge. I had very short labor with both of my children, but I won't say it wasn't painful. It was very hard work, but I felt like I was a total part of my children coming into the world, and I had control over what was happening to me the whole time.
>
> F. P. was wonderful . . . he did it all, coaching me throughout my labor. He was very involved through the entire process, and, afterward, I told him how much it meant to me to have his support. It was such a positive, joyful event for us both.
>
> As soon as Zachariah was born, I couldn't wait to get pregnant again. I had the most glorious feeling after his birth, knowing that I had done that on my own with no drugs and at home in our little cabin. I am proud to say that my children were born naturally, and I feel a certain bond with pioneer women who had done the same many years before.

After Zachariah's birth, having their daughter, Sarah Carlin Phillips, who was born September 3, 1997, was "a piece of cake."

By then, Katie knew what to expect and didn't have to work as hard as she had with her son.

Katie says, "I worked so hard pushing with Zach but later learned how important it is to relax the body, and let nature take its course. The more a person relaxes, the more the uterus is able to do its job of pushing the baby out on its own."

I asked the Phillipsees if more children were in the picture, and they both agreed it was a distinct possibility, but they wanted to wait a bit so that they wouldn't have so many in the diaper stage at once. My last question was if they would recommend to others having children at home with a midwife. They replied with a resounding "yes!" Katie adds, "I've turned into a real home-birth advocate, but more than that, I think a woman needs to give birth with her decency intact. It is important to feel good about yourself when it's done and not be stripped of your womanhood by letting others make the decisions that will affect you. Whenever women are left alone to labor, they will have positive things to say."

(Note: Katie and F. P.'s third child, Jacob Koschara Phillips, was born at home on April 16, 1999.)

Debbie and Stan Horst; Lyndhurst, Virginia

For Debbie and Stan Horst, having their second child at home with a competent midwife proved to be a very rewarding experience. After having an unsatisfactory hospital birth with their first child, Kendall, Debbie, who was pregnant at the time, began talking to some friends at her church who had chosen to have their children at home with the help of a midwife. Each person she talked to had such positive things to say about home birth that she and Stan began to consider it. They were referred to Martha Rohrer of Dayton, who had successfully delivered many of their friends' babies. After their initial meeting, they felt very comfortable with her.

We felt like she was very thorough and even more importantly, a very warm and caring person, and that was the biggest thing that stood out to us compared to our hospital experience. She came to our home for each exam, which was so much more convenient for us. I was treated more like a person, and, although I was more nervous than Stan about what we were planning to do, Martha was very informative, and I felt prepared and ready when the time came for me to deliver. And she included Stan right from the beginning, telling him how important it was for me to have his support through my entire pregnancy and labor.

When our son, Kendall, was born, I wanted natural childbirth but went to a birthing suite at a hospital to have him. They were very busy that particular day; I think there were eleven babies being born, so I didn't have a lot of doctor and staff attention. I must say the nurse that was on duty was very kind to me and couldn't have been better, but basically I was put in a bed and had to stay there through the whole labor process. It was a very uncomfortable and strained environment.

The doctor came in right as I was delivering and stayed just long enough to stitch me up and then left. We had specifically asked that Stan be able to cut the cord, but when the time came, they just did it and never included him. A few days after I came home, I developed an infection and had to be rehospitalized.

For these reasons, the Horsts were excited about being able to stay in their own home when the time came for their daughter, Jordan Elizabeth, to be born. Things were much more relaxed, and the couple chose to have Debbie's parents and a close friend, who possibly could never have children of her own, there to take part in the miracle of birth.

Unlike the hospital, the Horsts found there were no restrictions in their own home. Debbie was free to get up and walk, to take a shower, and find a comfortable position to ease labor.

When the time finally came, Martha was called, along with her assistant, Kaye, who was a qualified midwife in her native country of Ireland. Debbie was impressed by the fact that with a midwife, things are slower and more personal. "Martha gave me her full attention, and she didn't have any place to run off to. She stayed with me through the whole labor and birth but also gave us time to be together as a family. She had a calming influence which passed on to us, and she was here checking me from time to time, but for the most part, she and Kaye were very unobtrusive."

Debbie and Stan Horst with their children, Jordan and Kendall

As with most home births, Debbie was only in labor for four hours after her water broke. Stan participated by giving Debbie backrubs, ice chips, and words of comfort that only a husband can give his wife at a time like this. When Jordan was born, Stan was allowed to cut the cord and was then presented with his new daughter, who had been wrapped in a towel.

He says of the experience: "It was a very exciting time for me. Words can't begin to describe it . . . only that it's a warm and emotional time together. Too many times we make birth more technical than it really is. God designed it to work—and it works!"

Newborn Jordan was then passed to Debbie's father, Stan Shirk, which Debbie feels makes the bonding process even deeper than a normal hospital birth, where the infant is sent directly to the nursery.

After the family had had a little time together, Debbie was helped into a warm herbal bath designed to make the mother and newborn feel good and to aide in the healing of tissues. Debbie said

Jordan's umbilical cord fell off in record time, which she attributes to the healing waters of the herbal bath. Stan smiles at the memory of putting the screaming infant into the water and watching her instantly relax and even smile at the pleasant feeling of being in the buoyant solution, much like the amniotic fluid of the womb.

After Jordan's birth (the 913th baby for Martha), she was weighed and her tiny footprints were stamped on a certificate. Martha gave the parents all types of literature to read and took care of registering the birth certificate. She also did little extras, such as putting the birth announcement in the newspaper. She came back the next day to make sure mother and child were doing fine, then referred them to their regular pediatrician for shots and future checkups.

When asked if they would do it again, Debbie and Stan gave a resounding, "Absolutely! We wouldn't do it any other way." Debbie said even in the throes of hard labor, she never once wished she was anywhere else.

"I was just so comfortable in my own home, surrounded by the people I love."

MIDWIFE DELIVERY, FIFTY YEARS AGO
Marie Campbell; Lyndhurst, Virginia

Even though Marie Campbell had a midwife deliver her first two children fifty years ago, the reason why she didn't want to go to a hospital for her births hasn't changed in all those years. They are the same reasons why many modern-day women are electing to have children in the comfort of their own homes: privacy, comfort, and the presence of loved ones during one of life's most intimate moments.

Marie's husband, Gordon, had just gotten out of the military, and they were living in the Lyndhurst home where she was raised. Her parents, Lena and Killie Coffey, had built a small country store with a four-room apartment attached to it; they were staying there, letting the young couple live in their former home.

Marie was expecting their first child, and, when she went into labor, Gordon had to ride to Waynesboro to get in touch with Dr. Weems because they had no telephone. The doctor said that he would meet them at the hospital, but Marie's labor was quick and there was no time to make the trip. Gordon's sister Kathleen had come to the house, and Marie asked her if she'd ride down to Gertrude Harris's house and bring her back. Mrs. Harris was a midwife who luckily lived just down the road from the Campbells. The women were friends, and Marie said that it felt perfectly natural for Mrs. Harris to be there for the birth. "She told me everything to do and what would be happening the whole time, so I wasn't a bit nervous or scared, even though it was my first time giving birth," recalls Marie. "It was all very natural, and I didn't have any problems at all."

It wasn't long before their first son, Mike, was born. Dr. Weems drove out later that night to check on the new mother and child and found them both to be doing fine, and, afterward, he continued to be the baby's doctor.

Marie said that back then, midwives came to the house just for the birth and did not give monthly prenatal care. But because things went so swiftly and easily with Mrs. Harris, when Marie became pregnant with her second child, she decided to have the new baby at home and let Gertrude deliver that one as well.

Marie Campbell

When Vickie was born, Marie's sister Annie and her husband, Robert, were living with them until the house they were building was finished. Marie said that Mrs. Harris made sure that the family was included during the birth, especially Gordon, who was allowed to come in the room and support his wife with comforting words.

Marie said that she remembered that Mrs. Harris carried a little black bag with her instruments inside, and she brought padded sheets to put on the double bed to absorb moisture and the afterbirth. She came back several times to check on Marie and the baby, and her charge for services was a modest fifty dollars.

Mrs. Harris had a sister by the name of Mrs. Lyons who lived in Lyndhurst. She had the ability to heal thrush in children, so both women in the same family seemed to have the gift of a medical touch.

When the Campbells were expecting their third child, Dr. White came to the house and delivered baby Steve at home. Their next three children, Gail, Cindy, and Charlie, were born at the hospital.

When asked her opinion of whether having three of her children at home was a good experience, Marie was quick to say a very positive, "Oh, yes! Maybe it was because the midwife was a woman who knew how you felt, and maybe it was because you were more comfortable in your own home and didn't have the distraction of doctors and nurses you weren't familiar with coming in and out of your room. I don't know, it just seemed like everything was more natural having them at home."

Marie said that she remembered her family living in Sherando back on the wagon road at the old Vogel place, and a black midwife named Nancy Napier, who lived on Route 610, delivered her brother.

These days, Marie Campbell is retired and enjoying her huge family of six children, grandchildren, and great-grandchildren. I'd like to say a special thanks to Marie for letting me come and talk to her and providing her positive comments on having children the old-fashioned way fifty years ago.

Andy and Ann Segedi stirring the apple butter kettle

18

Apple Butter Boiling

Before moving to the Blue Ridge, our family was able to participate in one of the most popular fall activities that the mountains have to offer: apple butter boiling! It was a two-day event that was filled with a lot of work and the most fun I'd ever had. Plus the end result yielded a lick-your-lips product that went perfect on biscuits, peanut butter sandwiches, and even cakes.

We soon learned that making apple butter was a family thing as well as a church function, and most folks had in their possession a huge copper kettle that had been passed down through the generations in which to make the tasty butter. There were different sized kettles, but all were made pretty much the same.

Apple butter boilings have been a social event in the Blue Ridge as far back as anyone can remember. Because of the time involved in stirring the kettle and the close proximity of the two people needed to stir it, courting-age young people were more than willing to be active participants in the annual autumn ritual. More than one romance was kindled at the helm of a wooden apple butter stirrer, and amorous males would sometimes sneak more water into the brew to make the boil time last longer.

There was several little ditties about stirring that were recited while making apple butter to remind folks of the sequence needed to keep the product from burning. Two of them went like this:

"Once around the side, twice through the middle, keeps the apple butter, from stickin' to the kettle." This was the one Boyd and Gladys Coffey of Love used. The other one, used by John and Shirley Humphries of Stuarts Draft, was: "Three times across, and twice through the middle, steal a kiss at the apple butter kettle."

It was at Sonny and Bunny Stein's cabin that I first made apple butter. We drove up on a Friday afternoon from Richmond, where we lived at the time, just in time to help peel, core, and slice what felt like an endless sup-

The Bradley family making
apple butter in Montebello years ago

ply of apples. Actually, for one large forty-gallon kettle, it takes anywhere from eight to twelve bushels of apples—and all have to be prepared the night before the boiling. This process is sometimes known by its German term, "apple schnitzing" night. After the fruit is peeled, cored, and sliced, it is sprinkled with a little water and put into large plastic or metal containers that can be hoisted up and dumped into the waiting kettle early the next morning. I remember the men getting up before dawn to start the fire that would keep the kettle boiling. The kettle was either hung from a tripod by a chain or set into a metal stand that is made specifically to hold the kettle. But I have seen the big iron pot set into a half-barrel that has a trap door in the bottom that opens to allow wood to be put in.

Once the apple slices are in the kettle, water, apple cider, or grape juice is added to "start" the butter and keep the fruit from sticking to the bottom. Some folks use one gallon of liquid, others more. Boyd and Gladys Coffey always used homemade grape juice to start theirs, and it gave the butter a dark color and tangy taste that I found irresistible. Two pennies are sometimes added to the mix for the same reason. As the apple butter thickens up, the constant friction from the stirrer hitting the pennies and scraping the bottom keeps the butter from scorching.

Once the apple butter is started, it must be constantly stirred until it's ready to come off and be canned. The whole process takes most of the day, so it's best to have a lot of help with the stirring. The Steins had a little log cabin craft shop next to their house, so they always had an abundance of visitors, many of whom had never seen apple butter being made and who were more than willing to take a turn at the stirrer.

The apple butter is ready to be taken off and canned eight to fourteen hours after it has been started, depending on its consistency. About three hours before that time, all the fire is taken out from under the kettle, and anywhere from fifty to ninety pounds of sugar is added, along with several small bottles of pure cinnamon oil, and stirred into the mix. The amount of sugar to be added is a combination of personal taste and the type of apples used. The tarter the apple, the more sugar is needed.

When the cook-down is complete and the butter is thick and brown, the canning process begins. Lids and jars are kept in a large receptacle full of very hot water, and the glass canning jars are taken out and drained before the apple butter is ladled into them. Usually it's the men who scoop the butter out of the kettle with a saucepan into a large enamel canner or other type of container; this is then taken to the women who can the butter. Those scooping are on the lookout for those two pennies at the bottom; they will have turned bright and shiny from the acid in the apples. Once the jars are filled, the rims are wiped with a damp rag before the lids and rings are screwed on. No further processing is needed, since the hot jars seal as they cool.

The apple butter boiling down

John and Shirley Humphries stealing a kiss at the kettle

Cleanup is shared by all, and, no matter how it is done, it's the sweetest kind. Wooden spoons are licked clean by those dipping into the kettle for the "dregs." When the kettle is scraped clean, hot water is poured in with a little detergent and scoured down until the copper gleams. The kettle is then turned upside down and stored for its next use, along with the cleaned wooden stirrer.

When I interviewed John and Shirley Humphries at their annual apple-butter-making weekend in November 1996, they told me that from the eight and a half bushels of apples they put on to boil, the yield was somewhere around 110 quarts. I remember making a huge kettle with Boyd and Gladys Coffey at their Quonset hut up on Reed's Gap one year, and our two families carried home forty-eight quarts each. Needless to say, everyone on our list got apple butter for Christmas that year!

Here are two recipes for making the delicious treat; one came from Boyd and Gladys, the other was Hazel

Making apple butter in Montebello

Les Bridge samples the goods

Fitzgerald's mother's recipe. If you can locate a copper kettle, with a stand and stirrer, you might want to try a batch for yourself one crisp autumn day.

BOYD AND GLADYS COFFEY'S APPLE BUTTER RECIPE

6 bushels apples

1 gallon grape juice

50 pounds sugar

1 small bottle cinnamon oil

Prepare as detailed above.

ELIZA COFFEY CAMPBELL'S RECIPE FOR APPLE BUTTER

7½ bushels Winesap apples

7½ bushels Stayman apples

1½ gallons cold water

90 pounds (or more, according to taste) sugar

3 small bottles oil of cloves

3 bottles cinnamon oil

Peel, core, and slice apples. This will take about one day. Wash apples as slicing is completed, which will help the next morning. Early the next morning, wash out a sixty-gallon copper kettle and dry it. Place kettle in stand, pour in the water, and add one bushel of apples. Stir these apples until cooked up, then add another bushel and cook them up. Do this until all the apples are in the pot. Don't stop stirring the mixture, or it will stick to the bottom of the kettle and burn. After all the apples are in the pot, cook for four hours at a hard boil.

Pull all the fire out from under the kettle and let the mixture cool down. Add the sugar slowly, stirring all the time. Be sure to taste for sweetness; more than ninety pounds of sugar

may need to be added, depending on
the ripeness and variety of apples.
Put the fire back under the kettle
and begin stirring faster. Let it come
to a boil and cook for another hour.
After the hour, pull the fire out again
and quickly add the oil of cloves and
cinnamon oil, stirring constantly.
Pack the finished apple butter in hot
canning jars and let them seal.

(Note: This recipe was given to *Backroads* by Eliza's daughter, Hazel Campbell
Fitzgerald.)

George Allen and Allen Chandler

19

Mountain Music

Manley Allen's, Clark's Ole Time Music Center, and Buttermilk Springs Barn

I t's not exactly bluegrass, and it's not country; what it is, is old time Appalachian mountain music. People still love the simple words and melodies that they grew up on and have passed down though the generations. I remember Margie Hatter of Tyro, Virginia, telling me that a man by the name of Cecil Sharp came through the remote hills and hollers of her area in the early 1900s, talking to people and writing down the words to ballads that they were familiar with.

In Lyle Campbell's book *Life in the Blue Ridge*, a more detailed account of Sharp's activities was mentioned in the chapter on music (page 225). Lyle records that during the years of World War I, 1916 to 1918, Sharp, who was a British authority on English folk songs, traveled the Southern Appalachians, gathering ballads and folk songs, which were published in 1932. Michael Yates's website documented that Sharp visited Albemarle, Nelson, and Rockbridge counties in April and May 1918, and he was especially successful at White Rock and Nellysford. Dol Small of Nellysford provided Sharp with several songs. Buck Harris told Lyle that at White Rock, Sharp's visit is still remembered. He not only visited Alex Coffey and Philander Fitzgerald, but also spent a good bit of time with the Andy Allen family. A few of the Nelson County ballads Sharp published can be found on pages 3 to 6 of the Nelson County Heritage book, but no mention of Sharp is given. A compilation of these songs is available in many libraries in a book called *English Folk Songs from the Southern Appalachians*. A few of Sharp's listings from around our vicinity are as follows:

> "Fair Margaret and Sweet William," version L, vol. 1, p. 143, sung by Lizzie Gibson, Crozet, April 26, 1918.
>
> "The Shooting of His Dear," version D, vol. 1, p. 330, sung by Florence Fitzgerald, Afton, April 27, 1918.
>
> "Lord Randal," version K, vol. 1, p. 44, sung by Ella Campbell, Buena Vista, May 1, 1918.
>
> "The Lowlands of Holland," vol. 1, p. 200, sung by Philander Fitzgerald, Nash, May 9, 1918.
>
> "Jack Went A-Sailing," version K, vol. 1, p. 392, sung by Alex Coffey, White Rock, May 10, 1918.
>
> "The Suffolk Miracle," version D, vol. 1, p. 264, sung by Adolphus Glenroy Small, Nellysford, May 22, 1918.
>
> "Awake! Awake!" version E, vol. 1, p. 361, sung by Napoleon Fitzgerald, Beech Grove, May 24, 1918.

It seems that most families in our area of the Blue Ridge had several members who were very accomplished musicians and played for dances, as well as for their own enjoyment. The standard instruments used for this type of music are banjo, mandolin, fiddle, upright bass, dobro, a multitude of guitars, and a sprinkling of other assorted smaller instruments, such as the harmonica, juice harp, bones, and spoons. In our own family, my husband (Billy), his father (Saylor), our two sons (Mike and David), and our youngest daughter (Rebecca) play some type of musical instrument. Just getting together to sing and play was something we all enjoyed here at the cabin. I remember one instance when we were sitting on the front porch "scrubbing one off," as our son Mike likes to say, and singing all kinds of gospel songs. We didn't know that anyone else was listening until we stopped to take a break and heard clapping. We looked across the road to our neighbor's house and saw them sitting on the porch waving at us. We all had a good laugh and continued to play on.

Another family renowned for their musical abilities was the Allen clan. I remember Johnny Coffey telling me about two Allen sisters who played fiddles in harmony so beautifully that it brought tears to his eyes. Even today, the Allens continue the tradition of playing mountain music whenever they gather. Family reunions, church homecomings, birthdays, and pig roasts are just a few places you can hear the Allen family sing the old time tunes, such as "Dinah's Quilting Party," "Red Wing," "Barbara Allen," and "Golden Slippers."

In addition to folks congregating in homes to play and sing, there are three places in our vicinity that host weekly get-togethers where everyone is welcome to join in or simply come to listen to the music and visit with friends. All three are family-oriented functions, full of fun and a fair share of dancing for young and old. The only thing required is that you bring some type of covered dish, finger food, or soft drink to share with the crowd. There is no alcohol sold or allowed on premises, making it a wholesome, safe place for children and adults.

MANLEY ALLEN'S

The first of the three places is Manley and Betty Allen's house. They hold a get-together every Tuesday evening from around seven thirty until everyone decides to clear out. About 1987, the Allens started hosting the functions in their home, but soon the crowds became so big that they had to clean out their large garage/workshop to house all the musicians. In the beginning, just Buck McClung, Junior Lawhorne, Manley, George, Gary, and Glenn Allen would come to play together. But word spread, and soon folks were coming from as far away as Richmond, Lexington, Covesville, and Washington, DC; even two state troopers would drive over from West Virginia and back each Tuesday night.

Some of the better-known musicians, such as Jim Orange, Geoff Stellings, and Jeff Huss, who are master banjo and guitar makers, came out to play. One night, country singer Marty Brown, who was befriended at the local Walmart by Allen's daughter, Monica, was brought back for the evening's festivities. Betty Allen proudly

Playing bluegrass music at Manley Allen's

showed me the note he later wrote to them, saying how much he had enjoyed his visit. It was also rumored that Bill Monroe, father of bluegrass music, was aware of the goings on at the Allen garage and would like to make a trip in the near future if his health permits.

I asked Manley if the Tuesday music nights were cancelled during the winter months, and he said that because the demand was so great, he insulated the garage and put in a big woodstove so that they could continue in the worst of weather. If you want to be part of the fun, get in touch with the Allens at 540-337-4134 for directions, or just drive out to Allentown Lane on Route 608 in Stuarts Draft, and drive to the end of the road. The music will be waiting for you!

CLARK'S OLE TIME MUSIC CENTER

While we were at Manley's one Tuesday night in 1995, we met a man by the name of Bruce Clark. Bruce is a direct descendant of Old Joe Clark (Bruce's grandfather's mother was Joe Clark's daughter) and a retired Assembly of God preacher who lives in Fairfield, Virginia. His family owns and operates the Clark Sawmill and Lum-

Bruce and Katherine Clark

ber Company, which also hosts a music get-together every Friday night from 7:00 p.m. until 11:00 p.m. Bruce says they play bluegrass but also a fair amount of country, gospel, and the old Southern tunes that everyone is familiar with.

They started out in the sawmill's office, a little log building where samples of wooden flooring were on display, which made a perfect dance floor for those wanting to do a little flat footing. That was in 1994, but like Manley, Bruce realized that the crowds were getting too big for the little building, so nine years later, renovations began on a larger, vacant building on the sawmill premises to create a permanent home for the Friday night music social.

On a foggy, rainy February 21, 2003, the opening of Clark's Ole Time Music Center took place. The inclement weather didn't dampen anyone's spirits, and folks had a hard time just finding a parking spot because the lot was filled to capacity.

As the official host, Bruce introduced us to his nine children and his new bride, Katherine, who is as warm and welcoming as her husband. White lights were strung throughout the building, while antique tools and Clark family memorabilia decorated the walls. A long table of food lined the back of the music center, and folks could help themselves during the evening. Up front, a group was playing on the massive stage while others danced to the music on the polished wooden floor. Opening night, three musical groups performed: The New Camp Mountain Boys, The Rockbridge Pickers, and the regular Sawmill Gang. Nearly two hundred people came out for the opening night ceremony. The senior person in attendance was Bruce himself, who belies his eighty-one years; the youngest in attendance was Bruce's great-grandson, Caleb Davis, at six weeks of age. The person coming from the farthest away was a young lady from Yugoslavia, who said they didn't have this type of music in her country, but by the look of things, she was having the time of her life!

Dancing at Clark's Ole Time Music Center

The Clarks are a big, happy family, and Bruce's nine children play a huge part in the music center's activities. Bruce was married to the late Reba Woods Clark for almost forty-six years before losing her to illness in 1992. On December 8, 2002, Bruce married a long-time friend, Katherine Jenkins, who has two daughters of her own. Combined, the Clarks now have eleven children, twelve grandchildren, and four great-grandchildren. Both families hosted a large wedding reception at the music center on March 14, 2003, in honor of Bruce and Katherine. The Midnight Ramblers Band played for the celebration.

At this writing (February 2010), the music at Clark's continues each Friday evening. If you'd like to come out and join them, you may call for more information at 540-377-2490.

BUTTERMILK SPRINGS BARN

A new purpose, as well as a complete renovation, was brought to an old Staunton, Virginia, dairy barn in 1998, making Buttermilk Springs Barn one of the hottest prospects for wholesome, down-home fun on the weekends. Billy and Millie Ruleman acquired the property where the barn stands and looked for a way to breathe new life into the old structure. Gary Dunlap, who is employed by Ruleman, took the couple out to Raphine one evening to enjoy the bluegrass music at Clark's Ole Time Music Center. While listening to the music and watching how much fun the folks were having, the Rulemans began to see a use for their dilapidated barn.

On February 1, 1998, construction began to restore the barn, dubbed Buttermilk Springs after the small branch of water by the same name that flows to the rear of the property. The first week, all that was accomplished was just cleaning out the rubble inside the building. Then 250 tons of stone and concrete were spread on the ground inside the barn to level up the floor. Wooden walls were sheet rocked and textured, ceiling fans installed, the roof painted, exterior siding put on, new doors and a heating system added, along with an outside deck. Carpet was laid, kitchen cabinets installed, and a large oak laminate floor was put down for dancing purposes. Ruleman's small idea soon ballooned into a very large project.

The work was finished and the doors were opened on July 11, 1998. About fifty people came out for the first Saturday night. The three bands that played were The Sawmill Gang, Shades of Grass, and Heaven's Mountain Band, all of which played a mixture of gospel and bluegrass music. Those wishing to find a wholesome place to have some fun on a Saturday night readily accepted the house rules of no alcohol, no smoking, and a strict 7:30 to 10:00 p.m. schedule. Although the crowd is usually made up of seniors, anyone

Buttermilk Springs Barn

is welcome to attend. Many bring their grandchildren and let them have a try at flat footing or clogging on the dance floor along with their grandparents. No admission is charged, but a hat is always passed around to take up a free-will offering for upkeep costs.

The barn is used for other purposes, as well. The Rulemans have had a wedding reception in it, and various church groups, Ruritan

A Valentine's Day dance at the barn

Clubs, and FFA chapters have had events there. Billy and I attended the Valentine's Day dance so that I could take pictures and write an article for the April 1999 *Backroads*. We were both impressed by the beautiful decorations and how everyone showed up wearing the color red. The barn had a cozy atmosphere, and everyone seemed to pitch in and help with whatever needed to be done. There were tables and chairs scattered around for folks to mingle or sit with friends. And, of course, there was a vast array of foodstuffs to choose from.

Directions are easy: just take West Beverley Street in Staunton to the first left past the Marquis Memorial Church, which is Straith Street. Go one mile, and the barn is on a hill on the left-hand side of the road. So if you want a Saturday night filled with good fellowship and old time music, head west in Staunton, Virginia, to Billy and Millie Ruleman's Buttermilk Springs Barn, where their motto is: "If your soul needs some uplifting and a little bit of fun, come on out to Buttermilk Springs, and enjoy the folks at the Barn!"

Wooden barrels at the Stein cabin in Love, Virginia

20

The Cooper Trade

In the February 2005 issue of *Backroads*, I interviewed Leslie Philmore Critzer, whose father owned and operated a cooper shop near Afton, Virginia. The senior Critzer taught his young son the trade, and Phil helped his father in the shop for many years. While talking, Phil reached back in his storehouse of memories to a time when the local cooper was a very important tradesman in the community.

Many people do not know what a cooper is much less the important product they produced. A cooper is a person who makes wooden barrels. The only working shop that I know of is in Colonial Williamsburg, where craftsmen still demonstrate how to construct them. These barrels were used to pack and ship apples until the 1930s when they were gradually replaced, first by baskets and, later, cardboard boxes.

Phil's father, Leslie Philmore Critzer, Sr., was a farmer and a cooper in the Avon area of Nelson County, Virginia, near Goodwin's Creek. The family lived on a three-hundred-acre farm that once belonged to the McGregor's. After their deaths, Leslie, Sr., was employed as a farm manager, working for the woman who had inherited the farm but running the farm as his own. He taught his only son the cooper trade early in life while Phil's six sisters learned the mechanics of running a home from their mother. Phil's grandfather, William Henry Critzer (born in 1849) was a wheelwright in the same area, and Phil said that he can remember wagons and buggies scattered all over the hill by their house, waiting for repairs by his grandfather.

Leslie Philmore Critzer, Jr., showing his painting of his father's cooper shop

The company of Higgs and Young were the overseers of all the cooper shops, employing men like Phil's father to assemble barrels for the area apple orchards. Higgs and Young would attend apple growers' meetings, estimating how many barrels would be needed for that year's harvest. They would then contact the various coopers and place orders. Phil said they could turn out between sixty and seventy barrels a day, with two coopers working one shop. The Critzer shop consisted of a good-sized wooden shed that housed the senior Critzer and his partner, Ed Willis; they worked together at two workstations inside the building. It was hot work in the summer months, and the barrels had to be assembled in between doing the rest of the farm work.

Phil started working in the shop with his dad at a very early age. He was so small that, at first, he stood inside the barrel to put the hoops on. Staves made up the curved body of a barrel, and they, along with the wooden lids, were made at the stave mill in Greenfield and brought in for assembling by the coopers. One of Phil's first jobs was to cut the wire off a bundle of staves with a hand adz and then count out eight flats of wood consisting of two staves each. He would then turn four of the flats upside down so that the barrel would be symmetrical. There were three barrels to a bundle of staves and three bushels of apples could be packed inside one barrel. The staves were usually made of ash, red gum, poplar, or pine.

Work hoops were temporary round oak frames that one placed around the staves after they were fitted together. The work hoops held the staves in place until the permanent hoops could be attached. The permanent hoops were made of flat strips of oak, much like the ones used for chair bottoms, only thicker. The strips were soaked overnight in water to make them more pliable and easier to shape. They were then placed around the barrel and nailed together with three tacks that were compressed with a clinching iron. For each barrel, there were six permanent hoops attached for strength: two "head hoops" placed close together at the top; two "bulge hoops" spread apart in the middle; then the barrel was turned upside-down, and two more "head hoops" would be attached to the other end.

When this process was completed, the barrel was placed in a semicircular cut-out in the work bench that would hold the barrel tight while two metal devices called the "chime" and "crow" would cut both a taper and a groove on the inside top and bottom of the barrel, making the indentations that the lids snapped into.

The next step was to place the barrel over a hot stove with gussets on the bottom end that kept the barrel positioned in the middle. The heat from the stove would shrink the wooden staves, making the barrel fit together tighter. The men wore long leather aprons to protect them from the rough wood and the heat as they lifted the barrel off the stove.

When both the lids were to be put in, the collar hoop was loosened a bit and a rope was wound around the barrel top and secured to the workbench while the top lid was snapped into its groove.

The hoop was then lowered back down and tightened into place. The procedure was repeated for the bottom lid. Phil said later, when the barrels were packed full of apples, they used a machine much like a wine press crank to tighten down the lids for shipping.

When a barrel was completed, it was hoisted out the shop window onto a wooden track that led to a warehouse down below. The barrels would roll into the warehouse where the men would stack them for the Higgs and Young truck drivers to pick up and deliver to the various orchards.

Phil said that each cooper had is own "mark" that was stamped on the barrel lid to identify the man who had made it. He said that his father's mark was a dollar sign ($).

If there was a large barrel order, the men would work on them as they could, always knocking off a half-day on Saturdays. During this time, shellac was wiped on the "work hoops" which had become slick and shiny during the week. The shellac added a rough surface to the hoops, making them stick to the staves better.

The Critzer Cooper Shop, now a storage shed

The Critzer Cooper Shop, along with five other shops in the Avon community, closed during the 1930s, after cardboard boxes replaced the wooden-barrel-making trade. All that's left of the former business is the wooden building along Goodwin Creek, which has been covered in corrugated metal to protect the exterior. Although it is now used as a storage shed by the owner, at one time there was a blacksmith shop operating there.

Leslie Philmore Critzer, Jr., will never forget his father's cooper shop or the important work that was done there. To capture those memories for all time, he painted two large oil paintings of the interior, showing every facet of the barrel-making trade. From the tools needed to fashion a handmade barrel, right down to the water and coal buckets that were kept under the workbench, Phil's nostalgic paintings portray an exact replica of the shop's interior. The first painting was done in 1960 and the other, which shows more detail, was finished in 1985. Both were painted from a photograph that Phil had taken inside his father's shop many years before.

Like so many other early trades, the work of the cooper is now long finished. But the sweet memories of that era will linger a lifetime for Leslie Philmore Critzer.

Raymond Fitzgerald and his dog Zsa-Zsa

21

Raymond Ralph Fitzgerald

Beech Grove, Virginia

In March 1983, Raymond wrote down his early memories of being born and raised in the little community of Beech Grove so that his family would have a record of his life. In 1987, he sent those written memories to *Backroads*, and I published them in the February, April, and May issues of the newspaper that same year. He said, "I just wanted to put down in writing some of the things I remember from the days when I was a boy and later, when I grew up. I wanted you to know something about the way things were during the hard times and what it was like to live in the mountains back then. I know I haven't put down everything, but [here are] some of the most important things in my memory for my family."

I was born on June 28, 1911, and named Raymond Ralph. My father, Napoleon D. Fitzgerald, and my mother, Rose Ella, already had two boys, Hoy and Tucker. Effie and Tommy were born later, and one baby died at birth.

Papa had been born and raised on Tye River. He and his first wife, Catherine Blackwell, had eleven children. They were Willie, Charlie, Jimmy, Liza, Cora, Lula, May, Gertrude, Renie, Addie, and Neely. When Catherine died, Papa married Rose Ella Taylor from Love, Virginia. Her husband had died, and she had two

children of her own, Mac and Daisy. The whole family settled
down on Beech Grove Road.

I remember Papa and Mama both being high-tempered . . . a
trait I inherited, too. But when I was about twenty-one, I decided
I better change before someone killed me.

When I was a boy, we all helped work the family farm. Our land
started at the foot of the mountain with corn and meadow oak
grass and ended at the top of the mountain with an apple orchard.
The grass seed and apples were sold to help provide for the family.

We boys went to school as much as we could, but Effie was the
only one who could go regular. In the wintertime, the creek would
freeze over, and we could walk
across it almost any place we
wanted. Buck Rodes had an ice-
house dug and kept chunks of ice
cut out of the creek to be used
when summer came. When I was
about five years old, I broke my
leg scooting around on the ice.
My nephew, Clyde Fitzgerald, was
a lot older than me, and he came
over to do some plowing for Papa.
He would pick me up and move
me from place to place so I could
be near where he was working.
We were great friends. When

Raymond and his niece Hallie Taylor

Clyde went away to the army in 1917, he came by to tell Papa
goodbye. Papa told him to be a good boy, and Clyde said, "I'll be
back." He did come back and later married Daisy Henderson and
had two children, Evangeline and Hazel. I still have an old tobacco
box Clyde gave me when he left.

Papa was crippled later in life when his buggy turned over. He
had to walk on crutches for the rest of his life. He used to take us
boys out to the mountains and show us where to cut down trees he
needed for making chair bottoms. We would cut down the trees,
bust them up, and haul them to the buggy. Papa was real handy

working with wood. Bruce Anderson was building a new schoolhouse, and Papa made the shingles out of the chestnut trees that grew everywhere. We would carry his dinner up the mountain where he was working. We had to walk barefoot through the sand briers. The shoes we wore every day had long since worn out, and we saved our good shoes to wear on Sunday. One day, we found my half-sister's missing hen under a pile of Papa's shavings, setting on a nest of fifteen eggs.

We made trips to Waynesboro by buggy once or twice a year for supplies and clothes. Papa would leave about four o'clock in the morning and get home around eleven o'clock that night. But we'd all sit up until he came in. It was just like Christmas!

The horse and buggy was the main way of traveling back then. There was a buggy shop in Waynesboro where Leggett's department store is today. Old and worn out buggies were traded for new or used ones. Sometimes a man would have to soak a buggy wheel in water for two days so he could make the trip to Micah's Buggy Shop to trade.

Beech Grove road was about seven feet wide then; room for one buggy and no more. One time Papa and I were coming off Meadow Mountain with our horse Pete hitched to the buggy. Her colt, Nettie, was walking alongside. We met another buggy coming, along about Sliding Rock. Papa got out and backed his buggy up the bank to let the other get by. I walked up too close to the little filly, and she nearly stomped me to death. She had a bad habit of pushing and stomping, until she became the family horse later on.

The old Beech Grove road at one time passed in front of the Rode's house. Later it moved to the lower side. It went across what is now Route 151 and wound around through the countryside, coming out at Wintergreen Christian Church. In 1924, when the county began to widen the road, there were about six cars in Beech Grove. Saylor Campbell (Maphis's father) owned a 1911 model, Jerry Falls had a Model-T roadster coupe, and Bill Falls, Tom Hughes, Buck Rodes, and Kemper Ramsey all owned cars. Sometimes a month would pass before anyone saw a car come up the road. But cars didn't have enough power to cross over to Meadow Mountain, and horses had to be hitched up to a Model-T to get it across!

I made my first trip to Waynesboro in 1919 when I was eight years old. Papa and I rode across the mountain in an old truck owned by Eddie Dodd. Eddie's wife, Daisy, Ida Dodd, Pete Dodd, and Dorsey Falls all went along. The truck had solid rubber tires.

In those days, everybody went to church. We went to a church in Beech Grove that had been bought from another church. Later on, we bought a building that had been used by the Presbyterian Church, and that's where Beech Grove Christian Church meets today.

Courtesy of Peggy Ballowe

Petitt Coffey (left) and Raymond Fitzgerald

Every summer we would go up to Meadow Mountain Christian Church for a week of meetings. On the way there, we had to cross over the bottom pole of a gate, which was close to the ground. Mama got out of the buggy, but I was still sitting on the seat. When Papa tried to get the buggy across the pole, the wheel came down with a bump, the spring in the seat jumped, and I went flying about ten feet down the mountainside!

Joe White was the preacher for the meetings at the log church at Meadow Mountain. He had preached and preached that morning, and I was sitting there starving to death. There were about seven empty homemade benches between me and the people sitting in front. To pass the time, I started picking up the bench in front of me with my foot. I picked it up too high and it toppled over, knocking down all the other benches like dominoes. If you'd have set off dynamite, I don't believe it could have made any more noise. When the racket stopped, the preacher went on with his preaching and somehow or other I never got a whipping.

We had our share of problems as kids, too. We used to keep some steel traps in the back of the shed near the house. When we were just boys, Tucker and I were out in the shed one day, and Tucker decided to set some of the traps. He set one beside the door and went to get a second one. When he took his foot off the trap, it caught his finger and he started howling and jumping around and stepped right into the first trap and caught his big toe. My half-sister, Daisy, came running, and Tucker told her I had put the trap on his finger! I hadn't, but I sure was glad he stepped in that other trap.

Another time, Papa told Tucker and me to go out to the barn and turn the horse and cow out after a big snow. I had trouble opening the door because the snow was piled up against it and said, "The doggone thing won't come open." Tucker went in and told Papa I had cursed, and Papa nearly beat me to death.

In 1922, at the age of seventy-six, Papa died. There was about forty dollars in the house at the time, just enough to pay for Papa's burying. Later on, Tucker and Hoy went to Lynchburg to work in the shoe factory, and Effie, Tommy, and I were still at home with Mama.

In 1930, I went to Covesville to work at Ed Wayland's apple orchard and stayed with my half-sister Cora. The apple crop froze that year, so I came back to Mama's with no job. I went back to the orchard in 1932, making a dollar a day and paying thirty cents room and board to Cora.

But in 1933, really hard times came. There was no work, no food, and no jobs. I walked to Covesville and tried to get hired at the orchard, but there was no work available. Cora took me to the store and bought seven dollars worth of groceries and brought me back to Mama's. The next week, I was able to get a job at the orchard with no pay, but all the food I needed was provided at the commissary at the orchard.

In October of that same year, I signed up to work at the CCC Camp for six months. We built roads, tore down buildings, and cleared mountainsides, making way for the Skyline Drive. I made thirty dollars a month and sent twenty-five home to Mama.

These years were known as "Hoover Times," and a lot of people lost their homes and bought them back after Roosevelt was
elected. Things began to get better when Roosevelt shut the banks,
put all the gold back, and made green money for the gold. He put
ceiling prices on things and started CCC Camps for getting the
men back to work.

In 1936, I bought my first truck, a 1930 Model-A panel truck
from Paul Freed Garage. I went with thirty-five cents in my pocket
and a black heifer calf worth about twenty-five dollars. The truck
cost eighty-five dollars, so I traded the heifer, licensed the truck
with a borrowed license, and came home with the thirty-five cents
still in my pocket! I paid the truck off in monthly installments.

By 1940, all my brothers and my sister had married. Tucker to
Cora, Hoy to Lillie, Effie to Clyde Hicks, and Tommy to Ruth. I
was still living at home. At times between 1939 and 1941, I
worked on the Skyline Drive. My boss told me one day he was
going to see to it that I got married. I told him the only way I'd ever
get married was to find a girl back in the mountains where you had
to walk a mile and a half to get to her house, she could only have
one dress and one pair of shoes. He told me that if a woman like
that could be found, I would find her!

Morty Fitzgerald had moved over to Fresh Water Cove, and I'd
promised Eddie Dodd to take him over to visit Morty and his wife
Estelle. One Sunday morning, I was out in the yard when I saw
Eddie coming down the road. I went in and told Mama I was going
to take Eddie over to see Morty.

While we were visiting, Estelle told me about a girl she knew
who lived up on the mountain. Estelle went with me up the road
to where there was a turn off. She told me to stop and then said,
"Now what are you hunting for . . . a good time or a good wife?" I
told her I didn't know. She replied, "If you're lookin' for a good
time, there are plenty of girls that live down this road. But if you're
huntin' for a wife, I advise you to go up on this mountain." Well,
do you know, I went up on that mountain.

It was a mile and a half to walk up there, no lie about that! We
went up there that evening, and I met Bessie. She lived with her

cousin, Alice Bessie Brent Terry, whom we called "Big Bessie," who had raised her. Then we walked over the ridge to visit with John Johnson. Bessie went along, but she didn't have much to say. It was getting late, so I said, "The reason I'm up here is to try and get you."

Bessie asked me when I was coming back. I told her it would be about three weeks, but in two weeks I went to the foot of her mountain to meet her to go to church. She and her cousin, Liza Jane, and I went to church together.

I went back over there to see her quite a few times after that, but one evening I made up my mind that I had walked that mountain for the last time. We had talked about getting married, so that evening we were sitting out by the road, and I told Bessie if she wanted to get married, we'd get married, but I wasn't walking that mountain again!

Raymond and his wife, Bessie, in 1948 at their house in Beech Grove

Courtesy of Peggy Ballowe

Raymond with his mother, Rose Ella (left),
and "Big Bessie" Terry

On September 13, 1941, Bessie and I were married in Chester-field, South Carolina. Alice Bessie Harris became Mrs. Raymond Ralph Fitzgerald. She had lived one and a half miles up on the side of a mountain. She owned one pair of shoes but had two dresses.

That first year we lived with Mama. Then we built a three-room house and added to it as our family grew. Dorothy Mae was born on June 8, 1942; Barbara Ruth on January 14, 1944; David Lee on November 24, 1946; and Raymond Ralph, Jr., on November 29, 1948. We now have ten grandchildren.

Mama died on February 18, 1960, of leukemia.

Many changes have taken place since the days I've talked about. Where there was once only a walking path where the bear, deer, and other wildlife provided good hunting is now the Wintergreen Ski Resort. In many ways, that has been a real help to our family, and I'm glad I got to work there for two seasons. Of course, the road is very busy today with trucks, cars, and buses, but that's all part of the change taking place.

I just wanted to let you know how things used to be. . . .

(Note: On March 23, 1987, Raymond Ralph Fitzgerald passed away, taking with him all the precious memories of his early life in Beech Grove. What foresight he had to write his memories down on paper for his family. Because of Raymond's written words, we can enjoy for years to come the valuable legacy that he's given to each of us.)

Boyd Coffey with two of his bear dogs

22

Bear Hunting

A Blue Ridge Tradition

The mountains of the Blue Ridge are home to an abundance of wildlife, including the black bear. The men who live here carry on the tradition of the "hunt" just as their ancestors before them. Not only did hunting serve as a means of providing meat for the family table, but the challenge of pitting oneself against a large wild animal and the harsh elements of nature was instinctively in their blood. Today's men who hunt black bear aren't as hard pressed to bring home meat like their forefathers, but the challenge of the hunt remains as keen as ever.

Bear hunting is the biggest group-participation sport in the mountains. While deer, squirrel, and bird hunters seem to enjoy the solitary aspect of the sport, bear hunters thrive on each other's friendships, gearing up year after year for the activity that bonds them together like a tight weld. The men are a tough lot, seemingly oblivious to foul winter weather, blistered feet, and frozen hands. They are easily recognized by the dozen or more Bluetick, Redbone, Plot, and Walker hounds that they keep in the backyard.

Around the middle of November, talk is high around woodstoves at the country stores about how many bears will be taken and how big they'll be, according to the year's mast supply. Mast, for those of you who may not be familiar with the word, is a general term for nature's food supply, and that supply varies from year to year. Some years we are covered with acorns, walnuts, and hickory nuts. Other years, the nuts are scarce, and the bears have to forage more to put on the fat needed to get them through winter hibernation.

In our area, there are a multitude of hunt clubs and individuals who hunt together season after season. Wherever these men congregate, the names of old-time bear hunters are sure to pop up in conversation. Men like Maxie Campbell; Raymond Allen; Pete Falls; Wicky Stevens; Romey Fitzgerald; Ryland Jordan; Daniel Lawhorne; Ezra, Aubrey, and Elmer Carr; Wallace and Boyd Coffey; Curly Terrell; Clarence Campbell; and Floyd Weeks will always be remembered as the hardcore hunters who were out there, no matter the weather. You could always count on them to be in on the chase. Boyd Coffey always said that you had to be part dog to be a good bear hunter. He enjoyed being in the woods, watching and listening to his dogs, and enjoying the companionship of the other men. He and his group mostly hunted Cedar Cliffs and Big Levels on the west side of the mountain and to the east, Davis Creek, Wintergreen, Three Ridges, and the Priest.

A man who owns a good pack of dogs is many times the "driver," the one who turns the track dog loose and, when a bear is struck, is responsible for letting the other dogs off their tethers, too. He follows the dogs, hoping they will drive the bear up a tree or else run him by the other men who are on stands. Usually, a bear follows a predictable route through a certain area year after year. If a bear is killed, whoever made the kill gets to keep the hide, and the meat is divided among the men. You never get the full weight of the bear in meat alone, since the hide, bone, and entrails make up a lot of the body weight.

A good bear dog is essential to the hunt. Blue- and Redticks, Walkers, Plotts, and Redbones are some of the best breeds, but, for some reason, a cross-breed of the different types seem to work even better. One man said that he had a Redbone/Airedale cross that was the best bear dog he ever owned.

A big part of the sport is rounding up the dogs after the hunt. If you are hunting in your own vicinity, usually the dogs will find

The Boyd Coffey hunting party, Reed's Gap, Virginia

The Jesse Bridge hunting party, near Love, Virginia

their way back home. The animals seem to know instinctively that they will be picked up along the roadside when the chase is over, so they will make their way out of the woods to a road and simply hang around until their owners show up. Boyd Coffey used a conch shell horn that his dad, Wallace, gave him to call in his dogs after the hunt was over. He said that his dogs always came back to the sound of the horn if they were within hearing distance.

On an average chase, drivers will walk upwards of fifteen to twenty miles through the mountains. It is not a sport for the weak or fainthearted. I had the privilege of bear hunting with Boyd Coffey so that I could write an article about it for *Backroads* newspaper, and I could not believe what was involved physically. I found out from firsthand experience how hard it was to crawl on your hands and knees through an "ivory" thicket or climb hand over fist up the side of a rocky slope in zero degree weather. All this while lugging a backpack filled with drinking water and your lunch, along with a loaded rifle. Let me tell you, the men who hunt bear don't have a lot of insomnia problems after a day's exertions!

Jackie Lowery with a large bear he killed

The Allen hunting party, Stuarts Draft, Virginia

The Danny Stevens hunting party, Tyro, Virginia

I've had to smile at certain comments that I've heard over the years concerning how unfair it is to hunt bears with dogs. People who have no idea of what's involved in a chase, of course, usually make these comments. Let me assure you folks that the bear definitely has the advantage over the dogs. Not only does the bruin know the rough territory like the back of his hand . . . er, paw, but physically the bear outweighs the average bear dog four to one and isn't timid about using those teeth and razor sharp claws on a dog that ventures too close. Many is the animal that bears the scars of the hunt or loses its life in the process.

Boyd Coffey was a dear friend and neighbor of mine, and I knew him better than any of the other bear hunters, so when I interviewed him for the fall 1984 issue of *Backroads*, here's what he had to say about the sport:

I guess bear hunting got in my blood around 1946, after I came back from service. My daddy was a serious bear hunter from way back, and I guess it was bound to happen that I would be, too. All the old-time bear hunters would congregate up at our house, and Daddy knew all of them well. Back then, there were not hunting clubs, just men with a strong desire to get out in the woods and turn their dogs loose for the chase. You just picked a bunch of men to go with, and you went!

I grew up around the hardcore bear hunters like Raymond Allen, Clarence Campbell, Floyd Weeks, Pete Falls, Jesse Bridge, Maxie Campbell, and Curly Terrell. These were the true bear hunters. There was none of this turning over and going back to sleep if the weather was bad. They would be there no matter what. You could always count on them. I always liked being in the woods come hunting season. There's just something about being out there that sharpens the senses and makes you feel alive. Watching and listening for the dogs and enjoying the companionship of the other men have a lot to do with it, I guess.

We would get up at four o'clock in the morning and load the dogs, then drive to where we had planned to hunt for the day. Sometimes we'd hunt near Cedar Cliffs on the west side of the Blue Ridge and near where Wintergreen Ski Resort is now located over on the east side of the

Dennis and Raymond Allen with a bear in 1956

ridge. They ruined a lot of the good bear hunting when the resort was built over in Nelson County. That mountain up by Pryor's Camp and Black Rock fairly teemed with bears back then.

I've had upwards to eighteen grown dogs at home at one time, not including the puppies. When I hunt, I carry the conch shell horn my daddy gave me to call my dogs back if they get lost. They always come back if they are within hearing distance, but there are always a few I have to go back and call the next day. I once had a dog that found his way back home from Davis Creek three different times.

The photographs below are of two separate hunts from years ago. The first one, taken in 1957, shows a bear killed by Jesse Bridge that weighed 385 pounds.

Boyd Coffey blowing his conch shell horn to call in his dogs

When we started out that morning, there was a fine mist coming down. As the day wore on, the mist turned to raw sleet. I was driving the old panel truck and had to stop and put chains on it. Even so, I ended up tearing the bumper off and putting several good dents in the fender before we ever got the bear out. It was killed over at Black Rock in Wintergreen. The other photo was taken in 1949. Maphis Campbell killed the bear, and it weighed over 500 pounds. The men and all the dogs are lined up in front of the *News Virginian* office on Main Street in Waynesboro, Virginia.

Jesse Bridge with a nice-sized bear

On an average chase, the drivers will walk many miles through the moun- tains. I've had much younger men com- pletely give out on me. I had two fellas pester- ing me to go bear hunting, so I said, "Come on down, we can always use young blood on a hunt." They came from Winchester and were ripe and ready for anything. We walked and walked that day. They were supposed to stay for two days over at our hunting camp on Reed's Gap, but when I went over to check on them that night, they had packed up and were gone! I never saw them until the next July. One of them came up to me and thanked me for both hunts—the first and the last!

I can honestly say that I've enjoyed bear hunting through the years, but since I've become a Christian, I've enjoyed it even more. Now I can truly appreciate the beauty of God's creation instead of taking it for granted. I

The 1949 Campbell hunting party

always try to thank Him for the forest and the animals, and especially my health as I go out to hunt. God changed my life, and I give Him all the credit due Him for that miracle.

The next generation—Thomas Massie Huffman and his buddy K.T.

Down through the years, newer techniques and equipment have replaced much of the old ways of chasing bears, but as long as there are hearty mountain men, the tradition of bear hunting will never cease to exist here in the Blue Ridge Mountains of Virginia.

Peggy Campbell with a bear she took in 2009

23

Women Who Hunt

In the last decade, there has been an increase in the number of women who have decided to participate in the sport of hunting. Many have made the decision simply because they wanted to do something with their husbands, rather than just sitting at home and waiting for him to come out of the woods during hunting season. Others, like myself, have been hunting for years and know what enjoyment the sport brings. Not only is the meat that's harvested free of commercial additives, but just getting out of the rat race for a day and sitting quietly with my own thoughts is a surprisingly therapeutic activity. For me, it's the latter that I enjoy the most. But bagging a deer or some squirrels is the icing on the cake after sitting in the woods all day, knowing you are putting some mighty fine eatin' on the supper table.

In my area of the Blue Ridge Mountains, there is an abundance of women who know how to handle a gun and themselves while hunting. I remember a man asking me years ago if I was scared to be alone in the woods while squirrel hunting. I wondered what he was talking about and pressed him further; he replied, "Well aren't you afraid a man might try to bother you out there?" I burst out laughing and told him, "What man in his right mind would accost a woman sitting there with a loaded gun?"

Both my parents were city folks and had never even seen a gun up close. The closest I got as a child was one Christmas when I was twelve. All I wanted was a Red Ryder BB gun, to which my mother argued the standard line, "You'll shoot your eye out!" But my observant and indulgent dad, God love him, knew his tomboy daughter's heart and snuck one under the Christmas tree unbeknownst to my mom. I remember heated words between them late that night, but I guess my dad won out because I got to keep my Red Ryder lever-action BB gun—and both eyes are still intact!

My first experience with "real" guns came in my high school agriculture class, where I was the only girl in a class of sixty rural boys, most of whom had prior firearm knowledge. I begged them to let me try shooting the tin cans they had lined up in the pasture field, and I should have been more observant of the glint in their eyes and the smile on their faces when they said yes. They positioned me on the top of a ditch bank with the water directly behind and below me. Then one of the boys handed me a funny looking short-barreled gun and told me to aim at the cans and pull the trigger. They failed to inform me that the gun I was holding

Lynn Coffey with some squirrels

was a .12-gauge sawed-off shotgun, and I needed to hold it tight against my shoulder to avoid its powerful "kick." When the explosion happened, I was flung backward, over the edge of the ditch bank, and found myself sitting in water up to my waist. The boys were laughing their heads off, but the "little German" in me rose up, and I was determined to try again. The next time the gun went off, I was a little wiser; I stood on flat ground with the stock tight against my shoulder. The tin cans flew into the air, and I was hooked. I pleaded with the boys to take me hunting, and one insightful fellow realized that I was not going to be put off, so he patiently taught me the right way to handle a gun safely before taking me with him.

I started out rabbit hunting, then graduated to dove and quail, loving every minute of it and learning new recipes to try out at home with the animals I had taken. I never shot an animal if I didn't intend to eat it, and that stands true today. For those people who think it's terrible to shoot an innocent dove . . . obviously, you have never tried to shoot one! They are the wiliest of birds, dipping and diving through the sky, and if you do manage to get one, you've worked hard for your supper!

The first deer I killed was a whopper, weighing in at 187 pounds, field dressed. I was living alone at the time and was glad to have that much meat in the freezer. I ate venison every night for a year, following recipes in a wild game cookbook, as well as inventing a few of my own. The meat is free of fat, steroids, and the additives that are commonly used as preservatives in store-bought meat.

I guess my all-time favorite animal to hunt is the squirrel. I'd rather squirrel hunt than anything because the season opens in the fall when the weather isn't as cold as deer hunting, and you are pretty much assured of coming home with some game. Plus, if you've never eaten squirrel and gravy over hot biscuits, you have not lived! The next chapter in

Lynn with a nice eight-point buck

this book is on wild game recipes that I've used over the years; the one for squirrels and gravy is included.

Here on the mountain, most of my girlfriends hunt. Charlotte Hodge, who at one time chided me for hunting, would bang on pots and pans to warn off the squirrels whenever she'd see me heading for the woods. But in later years, she jumped on the hunting band wagon and is now a seasoned turkey hunter like her husband John.

Rebecca (Garris) Jones, who lived down the mountain from

Charlotte Hodge with a turkey that she bagged

me, bought herself a rifle and killed a doe deer the first autumn that I knew her. I have this vision of her that never fails to make me laugh. I was going to work one morning and as I passed her house, I noticed her standing on her porch in a flannel nightie, aiming a gun at something down in the pasture. When I got to work, I called her to ask what she was shooting at. She offered one word that needed no explanation . . . *groundhog!* Groundhogs are the blight of anyone who has cattle or horses in open fields. The groundhogs dig deep holes in the ground, which the livestock could very well fall into and break a leg. For that reason, mountain people have no mercy on groundhogs and kill every one they see. One summer, however, we live-trapped a young one with a glittery silver coat and transported it to another location because of his unusual coloration.

Young Kelsi Coffey, who is our across-the-road neighbor, began to hunt with her dad, Mike, at an early age and has brought home her share of deer. She is now a beautiful young lady about to graduate from high school and attend college in the fall, but she continues to enjoy hunting with her dad.

Jerry Lou Hanger got interested in hunting with a crossbow and has had good luck deer hunting on her and her husband Dennis's land, which is about a mile down the road from our cabin.

Our fifteen-year-old granddaughter, Renea, has also gotten interested in hunting in the last few years, and buying Christmas presents has been pretty easy for us grandparents since that time. All we have to do is purchase any type of cammo hunting attire, and she's happy! Although she's yet to kill her first deer, she's done pretty well with squirrels over at our Chicken Holler homeplace.

Kelsi Coffey with her eight-point buck

But the ultimate woman hunter in our neck of the woods is Peggy Campbell. Peggy is an original mountain woman, raised up on Spruce Creek in Nelson County, Virginia. The only girl in the family, Peggy learned to handle a gun early in life as she trooped through the woods in search of food for the table with her father and two brothers, James and John Wade. For the Campbell family back then, hunting wasn't sport; it was survival. Throughout her adult life, Peggy continued to hunt, and walking through her house, with the various animals she has mounted on the walls and floor, is like going to a museum.

Peggy does it all, hunting with compound bow, rifle, longbow, muzzleloader, crossbow, shotgun, and anything in between. She knows exactly what she's going after and usually comes home with it. She's our main source of meat production in the winter months, giving us venison and bear meat for the freezer whenever she gets something. But she's something of an anachronism in that while she does hunt, she has a tender heart towards all of God's creatures and seems to attract everything from young bears, turkeys, stray cats, and deer with her gentle demeanor. We've seen her scrape a clearing in deep snow with her tractor and put out food for the animals stranded in bad weather. Once, we came up to her house for a visit and watched as two young bears frolicked in her yard.

Peggy is the only person we know who has two strands of hot wire stretched around her house to keep the bears off the porch. She is one tough, independent lady who has the most generous, giving heart of anyone we've ever come in contact with, and her quiet but strong faith in God has endeared her to us forever.

There are many more women who enjoy the pleasure of hunting, but these are just a few in and around the Love area that I know personally.

Maggie and Carrie Allen, Stuarts Draft, Virginia

Elk in Estes Park, Colorado

24

Wild Game Recipes

Bear, Deer, Squirrel, Elk, Game Birds, and Rabbits

O
ver the many years I've hunted, I have developed numerous recipes for wild game and collected many from other sources. The recipes in my file are all tried and true and have stains all over them, which is a good indication that they have been used over and over again. Most of our meat diet is made up from animals that have been harvested, and I cannot even remember the last time I've bought any beef from the grocery store. Wild meat is very healthy and nutritious, without any steroids, additives, or preservatives.

People who say that they don't like wild meat because it tastes "strong" or "greasy" haven't learned how to cook it properly; perhaps these recipes will be of help if they have the nerve to try again. As the holidays roll around, our granddaughter Renea always asks, "Mumsie, are we going to have barbeque bear meat?" If we've been blessed with the gift of meat from one of the area bear hunters, I always try to save a large roast for Thanksgiving or Christmas so Renea will be happy. This is a powerful testimony for a taste test—you can't fool a kid!

BEAR MEAT
Barbecued Bear Meat

The number one important point to remember in cooking bear meat is to make sure that as much of the fat as possible is trimmed off the animal before cooking. Folks who complain that this meat is greasy probably had it prepared with too much fat left on. Remember, when bear season is in, the bruins have spent the whole summer stuffing themselves on nuts, berries, grubs, and an occasional raid on a bee hive (they really love honey!). By December, they are fat as ticks and getting ready to den up for the winter, so they have packed on plenty of weight; most of it in layers of fat. So trim it off painstakingly. Another hint is to pour off the cooking broth before serving. This will eliminate even more of the greasy effects it may have.

I have found the best way to cook a pot roast (plain or barbecued) is to place it in a Crock-Pot, add a small amount of water or a can of Campbell's French onion soup (no water added), and just let it cook on the low setting all day. If you plan to barbecue it, about an hour before serving, pour off the broth, slice the roast in chunks, and "pull" the meat apart. Then add your favorite barbecue sauce (or concoct your own), turn the crock-pot to high, and let it cook that last hour. Serve with mashed potatoes, vegetables, and fresh biscuits, and you've got yourself a hearty and delicious meal!

Bear Tenderloin with Pepper and Onions

This is another one of my impromptu recipes that not only tastes scrumptious but is easy to fix. I sauté fresh-cut slivers of onion and green or red bell peppers until soft and then set aside. While these are slowly cooking, I mix up a pan of white or brown rice and let it simmer twenty minutes, or until it's finished. Then I cut up the bear tenderloin into small, bite-sized pieces and fry it hot in a skillet with olive oil. When the meat is seared on both sides, add some water and Worcestershire sauce to the skillet, along with the onion/green pepper mixture, enough to make some broth. Heat through. Then take it off the stove and serve on top of a bed of rice. With a salad and French bread, this is one of our favorites! Venison tenderloin can be substituted for bear with the same delicious result.

DEER MEAT

Venison is probably the most popular meat with the mountain people (next to hog meat) because most of the men, along with a smattering of women, are hunters, and deer are plentiful in our area of the Blue Ridge. Deer meat doesn't have as much fat as bear, and the fat is easier to trim off. If venison were cooked like beef, you would be hard-pressed to tell the difference. Deer can be cooked a variety of ways, and here are just a few recipes from my personal file.

Venison Stew

4 cups cubed venison, seasoned with salt, pepper, garlic powder, and paprika

flour, enough to coat the meat

2 packages dry onion soup mix

8 cups water

assorted diced stewing vegetables (onions, carrots, potatoes, etc.)

steak sauce, to taste

milk / flour roux, for thickening

Toss the meat in a bag of flour until it is coated, then fry in hot oil in a skillet, scraping the bottom of the pan to keep the meat from sticking. When the venison is browned on all sides, put the meat into a soup pot and add the onion soup mix and water. Bring to a boil, then turn down the heat; cover and simmer on low for about one and a half hours. Scrape the bottom of the pot often. During the last hour of cooking, add vegetables and a couple of good shakes of steak sauce. Thicken with milk and flour that have been put into a Mason jar and shaken until well mixed. Serve with French bread and salad, and you've got a hearty meal.

Venison Chili

3 tablespoons cornstarch

2 tablespoons chili powder

1 teaspoon seasoning salt

1 teaspoon sugar

½ to 1 teaspoon cumin

1 teaspoon garlic powder

1 teaspoon whole oregano

½ teaspoon dried whole thyme

2 pounds ground venison

1 medium onion, chopped

1 8-ounce can tomato sauce

1 15½-ounce can chili beans, undrained

2¾ to 3¾ cups water

Combine first eight ingredients in a small bowl. Set aside. Combine venison and onion in a Dutch oven. Cook over medium heat until venison is browned, stirring to crumble. Drain. Add cornstarch/seasonings mixture, stirring until well blended. Add tomato sauce, beans, and two and three quarters cups of water, stirring well. Bring to a boil and cover. Reduce heat and simmer thirty minutes, stirring occasionally. Add water, if needed, to reach desired consistency. Makes about seven cups of chili.

Canned Venison

If you've never had deer meat that has been canned, you've missed a real taste treat. Canning not only tenderizes the meat but makes its own gravy, as well. If unexpected company comes, it's a quick and delicious meal that can be served up in short order. I got this recipe for canning venison from David Good years ago, and I still use it today. This is a cold pack method that is really simple, even for someone who's never done it before.

Before processing the meat, heat jar lids in boiling hot water. Fill clean canning jars half-full of cut up deer meat and press down lightly. Add one teaspoon of salt and a small piece of beef suet (fat). Finish filling the jars with meat, and place another piece of suet on top. Leave an inch of space at the top of each jar. Sprinkle one quarter teaspoon of black pepper over the top of the fat meat. Shake the water off the lids, place them on top of the jars, and screw bands down tight.

Place two quarts of warm water in a pressure canner, and put the jars of venison inside. Put the lid on the canner and process the meat at ten pounds for ninety minutes for quarts or seventy minutes for pints. Never add water to the meat in the jars—it will make its own. Thicker gravy can be made with milk and flour once the meat is taken out of the jars. Over a bed of rice or noodles, canned venison is a quick and easy meal anytime!

Poached Deer Hearts

Before everyone turns up their noses at this recipe, hear me out! There was a time in my life when I was pretty poor in the finance department, which sparked creativity in the kitchen. Since the area hunters were always butchering deer and discarding the "leftovers," I put the call out that I could use some "parts" if they were willing to give them to me. I received an abundance of livers and hearts, both of which are very tasty.

I remember one instance when my daughter was visiting, and Dickie Patterson came to the door with a bag of deer hearts. Heather just shook her head and said, "Mom, you are the only woman I know who is delighted to see a bag of bloody meat." Since I was always the one in my family who snagged the turkey heart at Thanksgiving and Christmas, I figured deer hearts had to be good. I have never seen a recipe for deer hearts in a cookbook, so this one is all my doing, but trust me, it is delicious!

Wash the hearts with cold water and cut down one side, opening up the central cavity. Cut out the white ligaments, then stuff with any type of dressing. Stove Top Stuffing will do if you don't want to go to the trouble of homemade. Lightly truss up the hearts to keep the stuffing from oozing out and then place in a pan with some canned beef broth. There should be enough broth to just hit the hearts halfway up. Slowly simmer until the hearts are fork-tender, then remove each one and place on a cutting board; slice them into "rounds." What you have for the supper table are circles of meat with stuffing in the center. I serve them with mashed potatoes and gravy that you can make from the leftover broth. Yum, yum!

Venison Pot Roast

Once again, you simply cook a deer pot roast like you would beef. I put mine in a Crock-Pot with a can of French onion soup (or a pack of dry onion soup and add a can of water) and cook on low for six to eight hours. I sprinkle a little garlic powder, salt, and pepper on it, too. If you want vegetables to go along with it, place them in the Crock-Pot during the last hour or two and turn up the heat to high. If you don't want vegetables and prefer to barbecue the meat, follow the same recipe as for barbecued bear meat. We love it both ways.

SQUIRREL MEAT
Squirrels and Gravy

To be perfectly honest, squirrel hunting is my very favorite sport come autumn. Unlike deer hunting, most likely you are going to come home with a few squirrels for your trouble. The meat is truly delicious, but it's the gravy that's to die for!

squirrels, 1–2 per person

salt and pepper, to taste

milk / flour roux, for thickening

After the squirrels are cleaned and quartered, or left whole, put them in a pot with just enough water to cover the meat. Sprinkle with salt and bring to a boil. Cover, reduce heat, and simmer until the meat is fork tender or falls off the bone. Remove meat from the pot and cool before deboning. Bring the broth to a boil, add salt and pepper, and thicken with roux until a nice consistency of gravy is obtained. Put the squirrel meat back in the gravy, heat through, and serve over hot, fresh-baked biscuits.

Fried Squirrel

Fry squirrels just as you would chicken, using the same coating. I always par-boil the meat until fork-tender before frying slow in a skillet of melted butter. Can't do no better!

ELK MEAT
Elk Steaks with Onion/Mushroom Gravy

I got this recipe from Jimmy Massie of Stuarts Draft who went elk hunting and was generous enough to share the delicious meat with us. Elk meat is really superb, and this recipe is easy enough for anyone to follow. Venison can be used if you don't have access to any elk. It's quite a long process, so you'll want to start in the morning if you want it done for dinner.

Steaks

4 pounds of elk steak, cut into 1½-inch thick individual servings

2½ teaspoons Accent

½ teaspoon onion salt

½ teaspoon garlic salt

½ teaspoon black pepper

3½ tablespoons cooking oil

Sprinkle the steaks on both sides with the Accent, garlic and onion salts, and pepper. Pierce the steaks with a fork several times so that the seasonings will leach down into the meat. Let steaks stand at room temperature for one hour. Then brown them in a skillet with the cooking oil. After browning, put the steaks on a plate until you make the gravy, but don't wash the skillet.

To make the gravy (ingredients next page), sauté the chopped onion until it is tender in the same skillet that the steaks were cooked in. Remove from heat and pour in the beef broth. Add the cornstarch to a small amount of cold water and stir until smooth. Add the cornstarch mixture to the broth, stirring well. Bring to a boil over medium heat,

Gravy
4 cups of beef broth

4 tablespoons corn-starch

1 large onion, chopped

1 large can mush-room pieces, drained

stirring constantly for one minute. Add the mushrooms to the gravy and remove from heat.

Put the steaks and mushroom/onion gravy in a Crock-Pot and cook for six to eight hours on low heat. Or you can cook them in a slow oven, making sure the meat is covered with foil while baking. This recipe is good served with mashed potatoes or hash browns. Serves up to six hungry hunters!

GAME BIRDS
Turkey, Grouse, Quail, and Dove

All four of these game birds are delicious, and the same recipes can be used for all of them, adjusting the time needed to cook, since turkeys and grouse have larger bodies. One year for Thanksgiving, I skipped the traditional turkey and cooked an abundance of quail for the holiday, and everyone was pleased with the delicious results. I'll give the basic recipe for that Thanksgiving meal, along with my grandmother Gockel's fabulous recipe for homemade stuffing, which can be used with a wild or domestic turkey.

After the entrails and feathers are removed from the bird, wash with clean water. Salt and pepper inside and out, and stuff with dressing.

For the quail and dove, wrap each bird with a slice of bacon and secure with a toothpick to keep in place. Place the birds in a greased casserole dish and add a few small pieces of butter on top of each. Bake in a 325-degree oven for about one and a half hours; bake the rest of the dressing, if any, in a separate casserole dish in the same oven. Cover the dressing and the birds with tin foil to keep in moisture.

For a fifteen- to twenty-pound turkey, stuff cavity with the dressing, cover and bake at 350 degrees for two hours, then turn oven down to 250 degrees and bake for two more hours.

The grouse is cooked the same way in a 350-degree oven for an hour to an hour and a half.

Anyone who hasn't eaten wild turkey, as opposed to a store-bought domestic turkey, will not believe the difference in taste. The wild turkey has an earthy, nutlike flavor that's unbeatable. Same goes for the grouse, quail, and dove.

Grandma Gockel's Bread Stuffing

This is the family recipe I've always used, and the dressing turns out moist and delicious every time. I've improvised over the years and have also added fresh oysters (cut in pieces) and different kinds of nuts, such as pecans and black walnuts. Any way you cook it, the stuffing is a perfect addition to a holiday meal.

½ pound bacon

1 cup diced celery

1 cup diced onion

1 large loaf sandwich bread, torn into pieces

4 eggs, well beaten

1 tablespoon dried parsley

1 can cream of chicken soup

Fry bacon until crisp. Take bacon out of the skillet (*do not* discard grease) and drain on paper towels. When cool, crumble into small pieces. Fry celery and onion in the bacon grease until translucent. Put bread into a large pan or bowl, and pour the celery/onion mixture and crumbled bacon pieces over it. Add eggs, parsley, and cream of chicken soup plus a can of water. Mix thoroughly and stuff cavities of desired fowl.

RABBIT MEAT
Bunny Rabbit Pot Pie

I made up this recipe when I didn't have a good plan for supper one night, and it turned out so good that I decided to share it with the *Backroads* readers. I used two fat bunnies for this recipe, but you can substitute any kind of meat you want with the same results.

2 rabbits

6 potatoes, cubed

2 medium onions, chunked

2 medium cans or packs of peas

2 cans cream of mushroom soup

milk

piecrust (recipe to follow)

salt and pepper, to taste

Boil the rabbits until fork tender; when cool, pick all the meat off the bones and put in a large mixing bowl. Add potatoes, onions, and peas. Put both cans of soup plus one can of milk into a saucepan, and heat until hot but not boiling. Pour this soup mixture over the meat and vegetables in the bowl. Stir until everything is covered. Line two nine-inch pie pans with dough and spoon the mixture into them. Cover both with the top layer of dough, and cut a few slits for the steam to escape. Bake at 350 degrees for one hour. You can cook them both at one time, or put one in the freezer for another day.

Piecrust

4 cups flour

½ cup cold water

1¾ cup Crisco shortening

1 egg

1 tablespoon vinegar

1 teaspoon salt

1 tablespoon sugar

Combine all ingredients to form a dough. Roll out to desired size.

Icem Lawhorne, Coxes Creek

Luther Cash driving his Hereford cattle

25

Driving Cattle

The Cash Family; Montebello, Virginia

A mountain custom that's still in practice is the driving of cattle from one pasture to another for the summer months. This is done to let the grass in the former fields grow tall and lush so that the farmers can make hay to feed their stock over the winter. I have stopped my vehicle many times while Jesse Bridge and his relatives drove his herd of Angus cows down the middle of Route 814. It was an amazing sight, and no one seemed to mind; rather, they were excited to witness an old-time tradition that you don't get to see too often in today's world.

Another family that continues to drive cattle to new grazing fields is the Cash family of Montebello, Virginia. Ralph and Doris Cash and their two sons, Luther and Stanley, along with a bevy of volunteers, make the spring cattle drive in May and again in the fall, moving the cattle back to pastures closer to home after the hay has been cut. The Cashes have continued this early practice for generations. In May 1999, they invited Billy and me to be a part of the drive.

In talking with Doris Cash, I learned that her grandparents, Hampton and Rose Fauber, used to drive their cattle all the way from Spotswood to their summer grazing grounds behind Mill Creek School near Montebello. Family and friends would walk alongside the cows and their calves, keeping them headed in the right direction on a trip that would take an entire day by foot.

In the 1940s, Doris's parents, Wilson and Ethna Seaman, continued driving cattle to the old Fauber homeplace. The drive went six miles from their farm located just past the Montebello Fish Hatchery to Mill Creek. As a child, Doris remembers the annual ritual and that their neighbors would come to help walk the cattle up to their land, known as the "Mag Field." She has been part of the tradition ever since.

In 1952, she married Ralph Cash, who laughs as he says, "It was because they needed more hands for the cattle drive." When their two sons, Luther and Stanley, came along, they also became part of the spring walk as soon as they were able to keep up. Four generations later, the Cash family continues to make the six-mile trip each spring.

The cattle know when it's time to leave for the summer grazing grounds. They start bawling and pacing the fence if they haven't been moved by the middle of May. One year, Doris recalls that the cattle apparently thought that the family was dragging its feet, and they left on their own. A call from a nearby neighbor told them that the herd was making its way down the road in front of their house, completely unattended but heading in the right direction. Several generations of the same herd of cattle have made the trip so many times that they know the way.

I was honored to have been included in the 1999 cattle drive so that I could not only write an article for *Backroads* but actually be a part of a spring rite that is fast disappearing in rural communities.

We met the morning of May 10 at Second Creek Farm, along with the other drovers participating in the drive. Standing at the cattle pen with Ralph and Doris were their son Luther and his wife Katherine, Lowell Humphreys, Darren Poole, Kenneth Fitzgerald, myself, and little Taylor Cash, son of Stanley and Kim Cash. Stanley met us later in his truck to help hold up traffic along Route 56 as the cattle were driven a short distance down the main road.

At four o'clock in the afternoon, sixteen cows and nine calves were turned out of the pen and pointed in the direction of the Mag Field, six miles away. Luther acted as lead drover, walking ahead of the cows a small distance to give them right direction. Darren,

Cattle drovers: (L–R) Ralph Cash, Darren Poole (with Taylor Cash), Kenneth Fitzgerald, Luther Cash, Doris Cash, Lowell Humphreys

Lowell, Kenneth, and I walked alongside and to the rear of the herd to keep them moving. Ralph, Doris, and Taylor drove their truck out to Route 56 where they would meet Stanley and help hold traffic when we crossed the paved road.

We walked the old logging road though the mountain behind the Cash farm until we came out on Route 686 (Painter Mountain Road). There we did our solid best to

Lowell Humphreys keeping the cattle in line

keep the cows moving down the gravel road instead of veering off over the bank in search of tall grass. There was a festive air as people living along the road came out on their porches to watch the procession and wave. A few minor roundups were necessary, but the cattle continued on at a brisk pace. They moved so fast that at several points, we were forced to jog along to keep up with them. Whenever they would get off course, someone would yell to Luther up ahead, and he'd call to the cattle to give them direction. Even with the mischievousness of the calves, everything went smoothly for the whole trip.

We worked our way up Painter's Mountain Road to Route 56, where Ralph, Doris, Stanley, and Taylor were waiting to hold up traffic. Down over the hill we went, turning right, then continuing down Zink's Mill School Road in front of Homer and Louise Anderson's house. The cattle began to slow their pace on the narrow gravel road, and we drovers didn't have to run to keep up anymore. We ultimately turned right onto Mill Creek School Road and headed to the high pasture at the end of the road.

We passed the old schoolhouse, which is still owned by the Cash family, and the home of Doris's grandparents. I have a special

Heading down Zink's Mill School Road

fondness for Mill Creek School because in the November 1984 issue of *Backroads*, I wrote a story about the reunion of the children who attended school there. There I first met Doris's parents, as well as many of her other relatives, all of whose friendships I cherish to this day.

Up the gravel road we walked, with the cows starting to bawl in recognition of the land they knew so well. As we reached the gate to the Mag Field, I looked at my watch and was amazed to see that the entire trip had only taken an hour and fifty minutes, cutting ten minutes off last year's time! As the cattle passed through the gate to the lush green fields they'd call home until autumn, I felt blessed to have been a part of a real old-time cattle drive.

Drinking Dr. Peppers and taking a much-needed break, we enjoyed the beauty of the day, surrounded by blue skies and bright warm sunshine. The men piled on the back of Stanley's pickup and headed back to the Cash farm; I stayed with Ralph, Doris, and Taylor, never realizing I was going to get another special treat before the day ended.

Doris was giving me a mini-lesson in Montebello history when Ralph told us to climb on the back of his pickup, and he'd drive us up to the top of the mountain, above where the cattle were now grazing. Up, up, up we went, on a narrow grassy cut along the side of the steep hill, with Doris showing me familiar landmarks across to Dowell's Ridge and Fork Mountain Road. The higher we got, the more spectacular the scenery became. At one point, the cattle looked like small specks down below as we climbed to the top of the ridge. When Ralph finally stopped, we were on the very top of a high grassy meadow, entirely surrounded by mountains. I felt like Heidi as she walked to the top of the world where her grandfather's goats were kept.

I realized what a privilege it was to be standing on such sacred ground with the wealth of history it contained. Doris told me that this land was named after an old woman by the name of Maggie Coffey, who lived on the property of her great-grandfather, Dave Fauber, and how Doris's family always referred to the land as the Mag Field.

The view from the top of the Mag Field

The spring day came to a wonderful close as the golden sun dipped behind the ridges, and the air became chilled. I thought about the rich storehouse of memories the Cash family must have, living their lives on the farm of their ancestors and keeping the old traditions alive in today's modern world. For preserving the past for future generations, I am in the Cash family's debt. You will always hold a special place in my heart.

Reed's Gap Road near Love, Virginia, 1983

Evelyn Campbell Painter, Irish Creek, Virginia

26

Evelyn Campbell Painter

Irish Creek, Virginia

To celebrate Evelyn Painter's eightieth birthday, Billy and I were invited to a party given by her seven children. Family and friends were there to wish this very special woman all of God's blessings and to express how much she meant to them. At a later date, we drove to Evelyn's home on Irish Creek to interview her for *Backroads* newspaper, and this story is the result of that visit. Read on to learn more about this incredible woman.

Evelyn with her children on her eightieth birthday

On April 25, 1920, Evelyn Campbell was the first of eight daughters and two sons born to Bernard Morris Campbell and Ethel Mabel Hite Campbell, whose homeplace was on Irish Creek. Her mother was the daughter of Leonard and Esther Barger Hite whose home was located at the junction of Routes 56 and 686, near Montebello.

Evelyn's siblings, in order of birth, were: Mabel, Margie, Annie, Mildred, Bernard, Jr., Samuel, Hilda, Betty, and Shelva.

The large Campbell family was raised in a large, single-story home that had four bedrooms, a huge kitchen, and a wraparound porch. Evelyn remembers that her parents had one bedroom, and all the children shared the other three, with wall-to-wall beds and floor pallets covered with straw ticks.

Evelyn's dad was a farmer who also cut timber and hired men with trucks in Irish Creek to haul the lumber to the mill in Buena Vista. Her mother gave new meaning to the phrase "full-time mother," making all her children's clothing and cooking for her large family. Evelyn, who is one of the best cooks I know, said that she learned to cook as a child while standing on a chair to reach the stove. She remembers her dad asking her to make him some sticky corn bread and cathead biscuits.

The family kept one cow for milk, and Evelyn and her sister Mabel had a good time churning butter in their mother's wooden churn. She still has the butter paddle and fancy mold that she packed the butter in for the family table.

They would forage for wild edibles, such as greens, mushrooms, and berries to make delicious side dishes and desserts.

They had two horses for plowing the garden and for hauling the timber they cut out of the mountains. They also kept cattle, chickens, and several hogs; the hogs were butchered late in the fall for the family's winter meat supply.

All the children had certain chores they were responsible for around the house, but they were also allowed time to play and just be kids. Evelyn said that she loved making playhouses and gathering moss from the woods to use as "spreads" for her toy beds.

The Campbell family walked to Ernest Grant's General Store,

close to their home on Irish Creek, to buy household staples such as coffee, sugar, salt, and flour. Evelyn remembers that she and her mother saved the brightly printed flour sacks the meal came in to make dresses for the girls in the family.

Evelyn and her siblings walked to three different schools. She started out in the little school at Norval's Flat, attending first through third grades there. She then went to the one-room schoolhouse alongside the road in Irish Creek, remembering that one of her teachers, a Miss Short, was not sparing where discipline was concerned. Although Evelyn never got spanked at school, she said that she spent time standing with her nose in the corner for one thing or another, mostly for talking out of turn. The children also walked six miles across the mountain to the school in Montebello, which was a larger, two-room building.

Her grandparents Leonard and Esther Hite lived in a house close to the school. She laughs at the memory of having to walk that far to attend school five days a week and then turn right around on Sunday and walk the same distance to church. She said that if you weren't fit before you started school, you certainly got that way by the time it was over! The Campbells attended the Brethren Church in the early years and Mount Paran Baptist Church in later years. Evelyn still attends Mount Paran today.

The family was very close, and Evelyn said that she can remember being spanked by her mother only a few times, mostly for going away from home and not telling her mother where she was going. Her father, Bernard, was a kind and gentle man who never raised a hand to any of his children.

Christmas in the Campbell family was celebrated with a special meal and the socks their parents had hung for each of their ten children were filled with small treats such as candy, an orange, and maybe a small toy. Evelyn says that nowadays, children have too many presents under the tree; Christmas should be a time for families to just be together. Growing up, most of the children who lived on Irish Creek knew their neighbors, even though there may have been miles between the houses. Clay and Nettie Carr were close friends and neighbors of the Campbells. Evelyn said that Nettie was a midwife and had the gift of being able to "take the fire out," which meant that she could heal any type of burn. Other neighbors included the Wheelers, Groves, Fitzgeralds, Painters, and many family members who lived along the Creek.

Evelyn especially remembers growing up with and always attending school with a boy by the name of Troy Kemper Painter. They started to court when Evelyn was around fifteen years old, and they dated for around three years. Evelyn said that Troy was kind of dragging his feet a bit, and she wanted to see if he really loved her as much as she loved him. So she told him that another boy was coming to see her in the daytime hours, while Troy always came in the evening. As expected, it made Troy jealous, and on June 18, 1938, the young couple was married in the parsonage by the preacher from Vesuvius Baptist Church. Evelyn wore a beautiful dress that she had ordered from the Spiegel catalog that she said had "every color of the rainbow in it." Troy looked handsome in a double-breasted suit. They both wore hats and white shoes.

From the parsonage, they boarded the train at Vesuvius and rode to Waynesboro, Virginia, where they stayed on a brief honeymoon at the home of her sister and brother-in-law, Mabel and Charles Truslow. Upon their return, they stayed for about a month with Evelyn's parents before Troy started construction on their own home on her parents' property. They lived near the "dinky railroad" that the logging companies had built through the mountains. Evelyn remembers that they bought a load of chestnut lumber for eleven dollars to build their first house, and the train brought it. The house consisted of two long rooms; later, they added a large kitchen. Four of their seven children were born in that particular house.

Evelyn and Troy on their wedding day, June 18, 1938

The Painters' children, in order of birth, are Roy, Joann, Roger, Boyd, Irene, Charles, and Leecy.

Evelyn and Troy's firstborn son, Troy, Jr., or "Roy" as they called him, was born at home. The midwife didn't make it in time, so the young couple delivered their baby by themselves, cutting the cord and tying it off with a piece of string that was taken off the lid of a jar of jelly that Evelyn had made the day before.

In 1949, the Painters bought the old Charlie Cash farm: seventy acres, with a house and outbuildings, that was right up the mountain from Evelyn's parents house. They moved all their belongings on a ground sled pulled by a horse. Evelyn laughs at the memory of the last load, carrying pigs and chickens, that overturned, spilling livestock all over the hills. "Troy ran all over, catching the pigs, while I chased all the chickens down," said Evelyn.

The Painters made a comfortable home in their new location, living the same country lifestyle as their ancestors. Evelyn said that she never minded carrying water from the spring or doing hard physical labor. They bought their first vehicle, a 1951 Studebaker truck, and would go off to church with all the kids piled

The Painter homeplace on Irish Creek

in the back or perhaps go get groceries or go to the Farm Bureau in Fairfield on the weekends. They never did own a car in their entire married life, opting instead for the trucks that could haul animal feed and the many things that a farm family needed to live.

Troy found work at the Tin Mine, which was located just down Irish Creek, a short distance from their home. Later on, he worked for the Public Roads Department, which was a division of the Blue

Ridge Parkway. He eventually got permanent employment with the Department of Interior (Blue Ridge Parkway) and served thirty years with them before retiring in the 1980s. He loved coon hunting and was a master rock layer, adding beautiful touches to their home with the chimneys, foundations, walls, and decorations that he fashioned out of stone.

Evelyn became very adept at cooking for her large family and enjoyed making quilts, hand-hooked rugs, and a variety of other intricate handwork.

The Painters raised their children in a loving home and everyone remains close, ribbing one another good naturedly whenever the occasion arises.

Troy passed away in March 1992 and lies peacefully in the Grant Cemetery, down Irish Creek Road below Mount Paran Baptist Church. Evelyn continued to stay in their home for about a year after Troy's death, then bought her son Boyd's home, which was located on the same property, just down the hill from her original homeplace. She resides there today, still having the luxury of walking to her former home anytime she wants.

The day Billy and I came for this interview, Evelyn took us on a walking tour of the home where she and her husband had spent so many

Billy Coffey and Evelyn inside her rock springhouse

happy years together. The old homeplace and the outbuildings that surround it are tucked back into the mountains in a beautiful setting, and a prettier spot is hard to find. I snapped a picture of Billy and Evelyn standing inside her springhouse, and I remember how happy she looked that day.

Of course it wouldn't have been a proper visit without Evelyn feeding us, and I can tell you, she did herself proud. Her table was filled with everything imaginable—from her famous slow-fried chicken and mashed potatoes to fresh-picked green beans made just the way mountain people know how to fix them to a plate of biscuits smeared liberally with Evelyn's homemade jelly. It was a feast that we enjoyed, along with her and her son Boyd's company.

Maude and Lertie, mountain women, 1986

27

Maude and Lertie

M aude and Lertie first appeared in the January 1987 issue of *Backroads*, a kind of poor man's Ann Landers advice to the lovelorn column with a mountain twist. Always trying to think of things to add a little spice to the newspaper, I talked my good friend and neighbor Charlotte Hodge into dressing up like an old woman with me and having her picture taken on Daisy Fitzgerald's front porch. Daisy and Carrie Fitzgerald really got into what Charlotte and I were doing and helped dress us up in some of their vintage clothing, as well as adding quilt batting to round out our bosoms and sprinkling our hair with talcum powder to make it look gray. At one point, Carrie got so enthusiastic with the powder, I thought I'd choke.

We started out writing our own letters and answering them in the column, but the whole thing sort of caught on, and soon we had "real" letters from "real" people coming in each month. We always answered them in a dorky way, which only fired the imaginations of those writing in; the column became so absurd that the readers came to love the homespun advice the ladies gave out and wouldn't let us quit. Maude and Lertie became so popular that many people actually thought I had somehow stumbled upon these two zany women on one of my many *Backroads* interviews. It got so that no one believed it was really us. We finally gave up trying to convince folks they weren't real and just went with it, providing

On Daisy's front porch, Reed's Gap, 1985

entertainment for a lot of people for several years. When the letters slowed down, we gradually phased Maude and Lertie out, but not before they stole the hearts of every *Backroads* reader.

Maude's persona, played by Charlotte, was a very pious, religious-minded Pollyanna, who wore rose-colored glasses and looked for the best of everybody in every situation. She was so good, in fact, that it made you cringe and feel guilty for being negative in any way. To counteract Maude's do-gooder personality, we added Miz Lertie into the mix. Lertie, who I had the pleasure of playing, was a blunt, acerbic, no-nonsense kind of person who annoyed everyone she came in contact with. Putting the two together, however, made them both bearable and amusing.

The following is a random sampling of the letters sent in to *Backroads* for the Maude and Lertie column.

Dear Maude and Lertie,
I've just about had it with "batching" it on my own. I am tired of

hot dogs and peanut butter and washing out my sox at the end of a long day at the mercantile. What I need is a helpmeet! I've worked up a few things, which I think would be a qualifying list of duties for an average wife. I'd like to know if you know any ladies who could fill the bill. Any leads would be greatly appreciated and promptly looked into. Thank you.
Sincerely,
L. Roebuck of Big Lick, VA

P. S. Here's my list: Must be able to milk a cow, churn butter, hoe a garden, can vegetables, wash sox, cook three hot meals a day, skin wild game, render lard, make soap, rub backs, look pretty, sing in the church choir, and have the desire to further the Roebuck family name by having lots of little "bucks." She must have a cheerful disposition and not be given to drinking wine or spirits. I don't want a nagger or complainer, but she can be between the ages of fifteen and sixty, as long as she has blonde hair and blue eyes.

Maude's Reply:

Dear L. R.,

I have taken the liberty to scout for any possible prospects in my lady's sewing circle, but the only available one was a bit on the thin side with a slight case of consumption, which would make her unfit for all the rigorous duties you have listed. Because I am totally sensitive to your need, I am posting a letter to my third cousin, twice removed, Estelle Zekely, over in Hicksville, to ask if she's interested in meeting you. Until then, continue with daily Bible readings and remember the Apostle Paul's words, "There is virtue in remaining unmarried."

Lertie's Reply:

Dear Mr. Roebuck,

How much did you say this job pays?

Dear Maude and Lertie,
My husband, Quincy, suffers from occasional bouts of chronic arthritis in his big toe. When he is in pain, I'm the one who suffers because of his constant complaining and outrageous demands

Maude and Lertie "takin' care of business"

on my time and good humor. The doctor has told him he should get up and move about to ease the discomfort, but he is content to sit in his overstuffed chair and bark orders to me like some old hound dog. What can I do to get him off my back and on his feet? Tired and exhausted wife

Lertie's Reply:

Dear tired and exhausted,

You poor thang, sounds like you been rode hard and put up wet! You've heard that old adage, "God helps them that helps themselves"? Well do yourself and that lazy scoundrel a favor and dump him out of that easy chair, boot him out the door, and tell him to "get on with it!" If that don't seem to get a rise out of him, tell him the medical field has come up with a new cure for arthritis of the big toe. It's called amputa-tion! That should get him movin' and hoppin' out the door.

Maude's Reply:

Lertie, Lertie, Lertie,

How many times do I have to tell you that you've got to be more sympathetic and compassionate to the people around you who have problems? Arthritis is a very painful condition, and I agree with the doctors that exercise is a good remedy for it. That's why I recommend that after his wife throws him out of that bloomin' chair, she should make him walk out the door (instead of booting him), and then remember to pray for him the rest of the week.

Dear Maude and Lertie,
I am nineteen years old and am concerned about a younger friend of mine who is illegally buying alcohol on a fake ID. The worst part is she won't face the fact that she has a big problem. As a friend, what can I do to help her?
Friend of a Boozer

Maude's Reply:

Dear Friend,

Drinking is not only a very serious problem for young people, but older folks as well. My advice is to stick by your friend and try to encourage her to get some help, even if it makes her mad. Tell her that you've heard that women who drink have a lot of wrinkles on their face, and they end up looking like a wrinkled up prune. If that doesn't appeal to her womanly vanity, then take some super glue, and stick it on all the corks!

P. S. One word of advice to the young men . . . stay away from strong drink 'cause I've heard it interferes with your manhood!

Lertie's Reply:

Dear Boozer's Friend,

More trouble has been wrought over the consumption of corn licker than any other thing I can think of. It makes normal folks do all sorts of things that they would never do otherwise. As an example of how "white lightning" can ruin your life, take my great uncle Burford. He used to frequent the cider barrel too often, get a real snootful, and mouth off to women who had big boyfriends. He'd wind up getting punched in the eye nearly every weekend. He never did get shed of the filthy habit, and when he died, they didn't have to embalm him because he was already pickled!

Uncle Burford's ultimate disgrace to the family was when he got so sauced he fell asleep in the outhouse and slid down the hole. What a mess! The men of the family had a terrible time fishing him out, and he ended up taking his yearly bath six months early. So you see, drinking can only lead to a stinkin' end!

Dear Maude and Lertie,
There is a good-looking man in my exercise class. How can I find out his marital status? I am single. By the way, we do our exercises in a swimming pool.
"Water Logged"

Maude's Reply:

Dear Water,
Personally speaking, I've always felt that mixed bathing is sinful, but since you are already in way over your head, here is some good advice: simply ask him, in a ladylike fashion, which of the other bathers is his wife.

Lertie's Reply:

Dear Logged,
For all her priggishness about mixed bathing, I'll have you know that I saw Maude hiding in the crabapple bushes down by the crick, craning her neck to get a good look at the boys who were skinny dipping there! Of course, that was about sixty-five years ago, but she still ain't all that lily white. In fact, it's my own belief that that's how her neck came to be so long . . . from all those years of craning it!

Anyway, back to your problem. I think you could just shade the truth a tad and tell the guy that while you were swimmin' around down there on the bottom of the pool you found a man's wedding band, and could it possibly be his? That should get the ball rollin'!

On the bridge at Daisy's place: (L—R) Carrie Fitzgerald,
Lynn Coffey (Lertie), Charlotte Hodge (Maude), Daisy Fitzgerald

Dear Maude and Lertie,

I am a teenager who has a big boy problem. I like this boy, but he
has a weird personality. One day, everything is just great, and the
next day, he's in a snit! I never know whether to talk to him or not
because his moods change so fast. What should I do?

Lonely in Lyndhurst

Maude's Reply:

Dear Lonely,

*I think you should just forget about this young man and go on to
some one a little more personable. Snit trouble is a serious business!
People with mood problems rarely get any better with age. Better to be
"Lonely in Lyndhurst" than "Stuck with a Snit"! Remember, "this too
shall pass," and you'll find someone special to spend your life with.*

P. S. Just what is a snit, anyway?

Lertie's Reply:

Dear Lonely in Lyndhurst,

If you are just in your teens, don't jump the gun and settle for the first fish in the crick. Be patient and wait for the right one to come along before you try to snag him. My third cousin, Gert, was going on sixteen and weren't married yet. She thought life was a passin' her by, so she grabbed the first fella moseying down the holler. She was sorry afterwards, too. Why I can hear her yet: "I hope your lot in life is a gonna be easier than mine," she said. "All my wedded days I've carried two burdens: Pa and the fire. Every time I've turned to look at one, the other had gone out!" So be willin' to wait, girl. Sometimes, all the early bird gets . . . is the snit!

Hallie Henderson, Love, Virginia, 1983

Wayne and Calvert Fitzgerald at their Fairfield mill

28

Fitzgerald Lumber Company

Calvert and Wayne Fitzgerald; Fairfield, Virginia

As a child of five, much of Calvert Fitzgerald's playtime consisted of digging in the ground with a mattock, loading up a little wagon with sticks, and pulling it to a make-believe sawmill. Even at that young age, he knew in his heart of hearts that one day he'd grow up and be a lumberman, just like his daddy. And dreams that are that much a part of a person have a way of coming true. Calvert, his younger brother Wayne, and their older brother Edgar are all in the lumber business and have been all their lives.

Five boys and one girl were born to Fulton and Della Snead Fitzgerald, who lived in Amherst County, Virginia, at the foot of Long Mountain. Fulton was a lumberman who had his own sawmill, and the children learned the trade at an early age, working alongside their father in every facet of the business.

In talking with Calvert and Wayne, they said that their dad would spend one week cutting logs from the forest, then sawing those same logs the next week at his mill. They recall going to the mountains to cut timber, and the truck would be so loaded down with saw logs that the boys would ride on the hood to put weight on the front of the vehicle so they could get out of the woods. Wayne smiles and says, "It's all we ever knew and we never wanted to do anything else." Their dad would take orders from various furniture factories for the dressed lumber and deliver it. The factories mostly bought oak and poplar wood to use as veneer on the furniture they manufactured. The boys rode along with their dad to Bassett Furniture in Bassett, Virginia, American Furniture in Martinsville, and Johnson-Carper in Roanoke. They admitted that both knew how to drive a stick-shift truck by the age of twelve but had to wait until they were each fifteen before they could get their driver's licenses and could go to work hauling lumber to the factories by themselves. One of the first trucks they remember driving was their dad's 1957 Ford F-600.

While we talked, Calvert and Wayne told a story about "Blackjack," the family dog that rode with them to the woods each day when they were cutting timber. On one trip, their brother Edgar had Blackjack in the truck while he delivered a load of logs to the paper mill in Lynchburg. After the transaction was finished, Edgar headed back home, forgetting that Blackjack had been with him. Two days later, someone called to tell the family that they had seen the dog at the traffic circle in Amherst, and the boys drove into town and picked him up. The distance from their home to the mill in Lynchburg was between eighteen to twenty miles away!

One tale led to another, and Calvert said that another time, they had gone to visit someone in Covington and brought home a cat that stayed with them for a few days before disappearing. Several months later, the folks where they got the cat called and said it had shown up back at their place. And people call them "dumb" animals. Talk about a God-given GPS system!

Fulton worked with his older son Edgar in the early 1950s, but later Edgar went out on his own, and at eighty-one years of age, continues to operate E. F. Fitzgerald Lumber Company in Amherst County.

Another son, Emory, logged and ran a sawmill between Massies Mill and Tyro for many years before he passed away.

Fulton had a portable sawmill that he transported to different places and set up where he was logging. Calvert remembers that in 1959, he set up the mill in a wooded area of Louisa called Bumpass, and he stayed there for two years while he cut timber.

In later years, the Fitzgeralds bought a hand-fed Frick mill that was owned and operated by John Mace in the city of Buena Vista. The next year, they put in an automatic mill which improved production, but a fire broke out and destroyed their chipper, and several floods caused a great deal of damage in the years that followed. The mill was located along the banks of the Maury River, and Calvert said that in 1985, a devastating flood washed way 300,000 foot of logs from the sawmill, but the men were able to recover 70 percent of the trees by simply going downstream, gathering them up, and hauling them back to the lumber yard.

In the late 1990s, the city of Buena Vista bought the property where Fitzgerald Lumber and Log Company, Inc., stood and began building a massive floodwall to protect the city from further flood damage. The Fitzgeralds then bought a piece of land away from the river, where Route 60 crosses the Blue Ridge Parkway and comes down into Buena Vista, and began construction on a new mill, where it continues to operate today. In addition to the full-service sawmill, a dry kiln was added in 2006–07, where finished lumber is stacked and dried before it is sold locally and worldwide. Calvert says that the kiln will dry oak boards in twenty-eight to thirty days and poplar boards in six to twelve days.

In 1976, Calvert and Wayne bought a sawmill in Fairfield that was owned by Manley Fitzgerald, and both brothers took turns driving back and forth from the main office in Buena Vista to get the new business underway. At the time they bought the Fairfield mill, it was operating by manpower, but by 1978–79, they had automated it. Calvert came to work full time at the Fairfield branch at the beginning of the 1980s, and, by 1985, the mill was running two shifts. The first shift ran from six o'clock in the morning until three thirty in the afternoon; the second shift operated from three thirty until two o'clock in the morning. Calvert said that for several years, he was there for both shifts. When I questioned him about only getting a couple hours sleep (at that time, he was still living in Buena Vista and had to make the drive home each night), Calvert said that it was hard, but, then, the Fitzgeralds are a tough lot.

While the double shifts were going on, the men employed

upwards of 120 people for both sawmills; that included truck drivers, office help, and kiln workers, as well as those who operated each phase of the sawmill. Currently, they employ about eighty workers at both businesses. A lot of the finished lumber is now exported to China, Viet Nam, Italy, and Japan to make furniture, some of which is then shipped back to the United States for resale.

While visiting the Fitzgerald Lumber Company in Fairfield, Virginia, we were given a tour of the entire mill and got to see, from start to finish, what happens to a sawn log once it is brought in on trucks by the loggers.

Unloading logs from a logging truck

Loading logs onto the log deck

After the logs are unloaded, they are inspected by a man who is known as a log scaler; he knows the worth of each and determines how much the logger will be paid per log. The trees are then sorted by species, and whatever type of wood is needed that day will be loaded on the "log deck" and fed into the debarker. This strips the outside bark from the trees, and the bark will then be made into mulch.

Logs going through the debarker

The logs are put on a conveyor and sent to the "head rig," where an operator running an automatic carriage slabs them off; that is, makes round logs into long rectangles. The slabs (the "waste" parts) are then sent to the chipper, which grinds them into chips or sawdust, all resalable by-products of the logs.

Then the "logs" are cut into boards. The boards are sent through a machine that cuts the edges off, and from there to the trim saw, which trims the ends off the cut lumber. The finished boards are then graded, stacked, and finally shipped to the mill in Buena Vista, where they are placed inside the dry kiln for a specific amount of time to remove excess moisture.

Sawing logs into boards

Grading the boards

Today's lumber operations are far different from how Calvert and Wayne's father ran his sawmill. Cross cut saws, cant hooks, and horsepower have long been replaced by modern equipment, making the lumber business faster, easier, less backbreaking work.

But in talking with the brothers, who are obviously very close, there is a hint of nostalgia in their voices for how it used to be.

The men are both strong Christians and are proud of the parents who raised them up to be active in church. "There was no question on Sunday morning as to whether or not we were going to church," said Wayne quietly. "We knew instinctively we'd be going." Many times after services were over, the family would drive over to Montebello to visit Loving and Helen Seaman, who ran the state fish hatchery.

It was a time when families were more in touch with one another, talking around the supper table and working the farm together. It was a slower time. A simpler time. A time when a five-year-old boy could dig in the ground with a mattock, load a little wagon with sticks, and pull them to a make-believe sawmill. . . .

The finished lumber

Burgess Ramsey Coffey at her home in White Rock

29

Lora Burgess Ramsey Coffey

White Rock, Virginia

There were certain people that I met over the twenty-five years that *Backroads* was published who had a special place in my heart, simply because I had more contact with them. Burgess was one of those people. I first met her and her sweet family at the Eli Coffey homeplace along the North Fork of the Tye River in a stretch known as White Rock. It's one of the prettiest settings imaginable, and whenever I'm over there, it takes me back to a time when White Rock was a bustling community, complete with a school, church, mills, and a few general stores, as well as a blacksmith shop.

Through Burgess's eyes, the now-quiet hamlet was suddenly alive with people who had died years before but still lived on in the vivid memories she passed on to me. Names like Holloway Coffey, the seven-foot-tall blacksmith who dated two women for forty years because he didn't want to offend either by asking one to marry him. Burgess told me the problem was settled on the day they buried one of the women, making Holloway's choice for a wife an easy one. He finally married Alice.

Burgess had a warm, welcoming smile that always drew people to her. Her soft-spoken voice and unforgettable laugh are forever etched in my mind, and I can still picture her face. She referred to me as "my girl," a term that always pricked at my heart and made me want to run up and squeeze her tight. When I had a total house fire in March 1986, Burgess called me up and said she had something for me. When I drove over to her daughter Margie Hatter's house, where Burgess was staying, I cried when she presented me with two blue handmade pillows with a note that read, "For my girl . . . these pillows are for you to lay your sweet head on." People were so generous after the fire, and I appreciated everything they did for me, but those two pillows that Burgess made for me represented all the Godly love she showed to everyone. I miss her to this day.

Her extended family continues to hold their family reunions at Eli Coffey's cabin, each year on the fourth Sunday in July. Members of the family tree still in the area include Ramsey, Coffey, Allen, Steele, and other branches come out to visit, catch up, reminisce, and compare early family photos. It was always such a treat for me to drive up the picturesque North Fork Road (Route 687, "closest thing to heaven," as Preacher Billy Morris used to say) to the Ramsey reunion, where I got to see Burgess and her huge family. I took their pictures and put them in *Backroads* newspaper the following month, and it seemed everyone looked forward to seeing who was going to be featured that particular year. Over the course of years, I felt like part of the family myself, and then in a twist of irony, I married Billy Coffey in 1993, and suddenly I became everyone's "cousin" by marriage!

Lora Burgess Ramsey was born on April 28, 1902, to William M. Ramsey and Serena Painter Ramsey, who lived at the bottom of a deep hollow under the shadow of Bald Mountain. She was told that her mama was in the field dropping corn on the day she was born. Burgess said that she worked in that same field from the time she was a young girl until she got married. Her father had six children with his first wife before she died, and then he had ten more after he married Burgess's mother.

As a child, Burgess said that she had a good life. Like so many of the mountain families, they lacked many of the material things in life but were very rich in the basics. Or as Burgess puts it, "I never looked at the money part of it. I had plenty to eat, plenty of clothes to wear; I had my health and my family's love, so how could a person be any richer?"

Courtesy of Lonne Allen and Lura Steele

Three of the Ramsey girls, prior to 1920: Mary (standing), and (L–R) Burgess and Lina

Although the children didn't receive gifts for their birthdays, their mama always baked each of them a cake. On her sixteenth birthday, however, Burgess was given a set of flatware, which she then used at the family table.

She met her future husband, Hercy Coffey, while still in her teens. He was a good friend of Burgess's brother and used to come home with him a lot. They courted for about two years before Hercy went into service, then another two years after he came home. After the couple married, they lived up the North Fork Road a few miles from White Rock, closer to where the Blue Ridge Parkway was to be constructed. Their next home was located just down from the White Rock School, where they opened a little store in the back of the house to supplement their farming income. Later the Coffeys moved into Hercy's parents' cabin, which had been vacant for several years because his folks had moved to a house in the Ladd area. Burgess and Hercy set up housekeeping in the cabin in June, but in the fall, his parents decided to move back, along with their son Tom and another son and his family. Burgess laughed when she said, "What a sight! Twelve of us living in that tiny cabin together."

Burgess said that in 1932, they built their own home right next to Eli Coffey's cabin. By that time, their family of three daughters was complete. Marjorie, Lura, and Lorine grew up in the white frame house that bordered the Tye River right in the heart of White Rock. Hercy borrowed money and built his own gristmill and later added a sawmill, which he operated. They again opened a small store, which was stocked with a little of everything. Burgess said that her husband always liked being his own boss. He tried working for someone else, but after just a short time, he tired of it, coming home and saying, "Never again!"

Burgess stayed at home and did what had to be done. She was an excellent seamstress and took in sewing for other people, as well as making all their daughters' clothes. She recalled that people often paid her in tomatoes and roasting ears for her work. And she once traded her older sister a handmade rocking chair for an old Minnesota sewing machine. She remembers that it made a long stitch that looked almost like a handmade quilting stitch.

Courtesy of Lorine Allen and Lura Steele

Stanley Ramsey and Hercy Coffey (back row); Velma Ramsey and Burgess Coffey (in front)

The family attended services at the White Rock Christian Church, just up the hill a ways. Reilly Fitzgerald was the first man to preach there. Preachers that followed were Davis Coffey, Pettit Coffey, and Emmett Perry. Burgess said that Ellwood Campbell, who was a favorite preacher from the area, preached his first sermon there. The congregation had great revivals back then, and the people would walk down from the mountains carrying lanterns to light their way home.

Burgess said that they had a good life back then, with virtually everything they needed right around their home. From a store and mill to a church and school and even a daily paper out of Lynchburg and mail service, the people of White Rock seemed to have it all.

I asked Burgess if she could recall any of the other families that lived around them, and, in an instant, she began reeling off names: RoseAnna and Edward Carr, Quincey Coffey, Mitchell Fitzgerald, Boston Taylor, Holloway Coffey, Eulie Fitzgerald, and many others. Just like it was yesterday, she reached back in her memory and counted off each family from the North Fork of the Tye River all the way up to Durham's Run.

Burgess's darling Hercy passed away in 1956, and she promised him that she wouldn't live by herself. So after his death, she began living with each of her three daughters at various times.

At the age of sixty-one, she decided to take up the art of oil painting, and much of her primitive art now hangs in the homes of family and friends. Burgess explained that Captain Billy Massie's mother is the one responsible for showing her how to paint. "One day when I was over visiting, I watched her and said, 'You know, I believe I could do that.' She encouraged me to try, and I just cleaned off an old canvas and started right in. When I had finished, I asked her what she thought. She looked at it for a bit and then said, 'I'm going to be honest with you

Hercy and Burgess with grandchildren Tonya Steele (in arms), Gary Allen, Ann Steele, Bobby Steele

Courtesy of Lorine Allen and Lura Steele

. . . it looks horrible!' But that didn't hurt my feelings at all, and I kept at it. Pretty soon, people couldn't tell my paintings from hers. My proudest piece was the picture I painted of my childhood home up on Bald Mountain. The old homeplace burned down in 1916, so I painted it completely from memory."

I finished up by asking Burgess if she felt as if she had had a good life all in all. She was quick to reply with a yes and laughed as she told me how she teases her preacher Billy Morris about being poor.

"When he starts in about how poor he used to be, I tell him that I never was poor. My daughter Margie always butts in and says, 'Oh, Mama, how could a person get any poorer?' But I never felt poor inside, and that's what counts."

Burgess on her front porch

Sitting with Burgess on the porch of Eli's log cabin, I pause to just look around for a moment. Those beautiful dark blue mountains loom above us, and just a stone's throw away, the waters of the rocky Tye River sing their sweet song. Here we are, sitting amongst God's unspoiled creation in a place that hasn't changed much in a hundred years. There is so much beauty to take in and so many memories to fondly look back on. No wonder Burgess thought she was rich—she *was!* The pure nostalgia of it wells up inside me and makes me homesick for a

Burgess Coffey's home at White Rock

life that I was never even a part of. I am so grateful for the little taste of it that I've been able to savor by knowing people like Burgess Coffey.

(Note: My sweet Burgess passed away on January 19, 1993, at ninety-one years of age. At her ninetieth birthday party, I asked her how she felt about living to be that old. She replied, "Honey, I never expected to make it to eighty much less ninety. Life has been very good to me, and God has blessed me so richly with a loving family and friends. Today was wonderful because it was a total surprise, which is a lot better than sitting around waiting for something to happen. . . .")

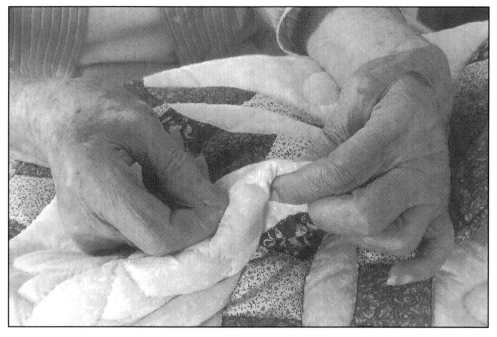

Vera Falls's hands as she makes a quilt

Mama's Mama

Mama's Mama, on a winter's day,
Milked the cows and fed them hay.
Slopped the hogs, saddled the mule,
And got the children off to school.
Did a washing, mopped the floors,
Washed the windows and did some chores.
Cooked a dish of home-dried fruit,
Pressed her husband's Sunday suit.
Swept the parlor, made the bed,
Baked a dozen loaves of bread.
Split some wood and lugged it in,
Enough to fill the kitchen bin.
Cleaned the lamps and put in oil,
Stewed some apples she thought would spoil.
Churned the butter, baked a cake,
Then exclaimed, "For mercy sake,
The calves have got out of the pen!"
Went out and chased them back again.
Gathered the eggs and locked the stable,
Returned to the house and set the table.
Cooked a supper that was delicious,
And afterwards washed all the dishes.
Fed the cat, sprinkled some clothes,
Mended a basketful of hose.
Then opened the organ and began to play,
"When You Come to the End of a Perfect Day."

—*Author unknown*

About the Author

Even as a child, Lynn Coffey had a Waldenish bent toward a nineteenth-century existence, despite the fact that she was growing up along the busy Gold Coast of southern Florida, with all the amenities of modern living. Her dream was to someday live in a log cabin in the mountains and live a quiet, self-sufficient lifestyle.

Lynn began living that dream upon moving to the tiny hamlet of Love, Virginia, in the summer of 1980. As she met and got to know her neighbors, all of whom were quite elderly at the time, she soon realized the culture of these hearty Scottish/Irish descendants was slowly vanishing and needed to be preserved.

Without any formal education or prior experience in journalism, Lynn carved out a folksy niche of documenting early Appalachian life through the pages of a monthly newspaper called *Backroads*, the first issue being published in December 1981. For the next twenty-five years, *Backroads* chronicled the history of the mountain people as Lynn traveled the hills and hollers, interviewing the elders and photographing handicrafts and activities that had been handed down for generations.

In the process, little did she realize how entwined their lives would become or how much the mountain people would come to mean to her as they opened their hearts to trust a young woman who started out as an "outsider" and ended up becoming one of them.

You can request additional copies of *Backroads 2* by using this order form.

ORDER FORM

Name _____

Address _____

City, State, Zip _____

Please send me _____ copies of *Backroads 2* at $20.00 each plus $5.00 per book shipping.

Make checks or money orders payable to Lynn Coffey and mail to:

Lynn Coffey
1461 Love Road
Lyndhurst, VA 22952

ORDER FORM

Name _____

Address _____

City, State, Zip _____

Please send me _____ copies of *Backroads 2* at $20.00 each plus $5.00 per book shipping.

Make checks or money orders payable to Lynn Coffey and mail to:

Lynn Coffey
1461 Love Road
Lyndhurst, VA 22952